御贈書草目録

穀類

粳米 一（ウルゴメ・サクゴメ）
糯米 二（モチゴメ）
火米 三（ギャマイ）
陳倉米 四（フルゴメ）
秈米 五（シラゴメ）
黍米 六（キビ）
稷米 七（ムギ）
黄粱米 八（モチアハ）
粟米 九（アハ）
大麥 十（オホムギ）
小麥 十一（コムギ）
蕎麥 十二（ソバムギ）
蜀黍 十三（キビ）
玉蜀黍 十四（ワウトウキビ）
落花生 十五（ラクヂセウ）
黒胡麻 十六（クロゴマ）
白胡麻 十七（シロゴマ）
鸚哥粟 十八（インコアハ）
大黒豆 十九（オホクロマメ）
黄大豆 二十（キダイヅ）

Traditional Cuisine of the Ryukyu Islands

A History of Health and Healing

TAKAGI Rin

Translated by ENDA Kazuko and Deborah Iwabuchi

Japan Publishing Industry Foundation for Culture

Tundābun

In the Ryukyu Kingdom, a *tundābun*—a type of lidded lacquerware tray—was used to serve court cuisine to distinguished guests. *Tundā* means "lord of the east," and *bun* means "tray." Such trays were exquisitely decorated with phoenix and dragon motifs in mother-of-pearl inlay work, and were divided into partitions to serve various sumptuous dishes that showed off the elegance of the Ryukyu dynasty. *Tundābun* trays are treasures of Ryukyu cuisine and its spirit of hospitality.

Pōpō

A crepe-like snack with *andansu* (miso mixed with sugar and pork fat) inside
→ pp. 62–63 wheat flour, *muginoko*

Kombu rolls

Parboiled fish wrapped in kombu and tied with a strip of *kanpyō* dried gourd
→ p. 94, kombu, *konbu*

Fried and simmered *ta-imo* taro root

Ta-imo (*tānmu*) fried simmered sweet taro root is indispensable as a celebratory dish. *Ta-imo* paste is neatly shaped, fried, and then simmered in soy sauce and sugar
→ p. 82 taro, *ta-imo*

Minudaru

Pork ribs dipped in a sauce of black sesame seeds, soy sauce, sugar, and mirin, then steamed
→ pp. 104–107 pork, *buta-shishi*

Buta no gobōmaki

Burdock root wrapped in pork roast and simmered in stock, soy sauce, *awamori* (a distilled rice liquor), and sugar
→ p. 104 pork, *buta-shishi*

Shishi-kamabuku

Cake of steamed fish and pork paste
→ p. 127 *kamoboko*, *kamaboku*

Green *kamabuku*

Bright-green *kamaboko* steamed fish paste with mugwort
→ p. 127 *kamoboko*, *kamaboku*

Chimu-machi

Steamed pork liver wrapped in caul fat
→ p. 109 pork liver, *buta-kimo*

Kubushime flowers (center)

Thick slices of *kubushime* cuttlefish are cut into designs requiring expert knife skills
→ p. 125 broadclub cuttlefish, *kubushime*

Note to readers
This book follows the Hepburn system of romanization. Except for place names found on international maps, as well as the Japanese names on the jacket, cover, and this page, long vowels are indicated by macrons. The tradition of placing the family name first has been followed for Japanese and Chinese names.

Traditional Cuisine of the Ryukyu Islands: A History of Health and Healing
by Takagi Rin. Translated by Enda Kazuko and Deborah Iwabuchi.

Published by
Japan Publishing Industry Foundation for Culture (JPIC)
2-2-30 Kanda-Jinbocho, Chiyoda-ku, Tokyo 101-0051, Japan

First English edition: March 2020

This book is a translation of *Dai Ryukyu ryori cho* which was originally published in 2009 by SHINCHOSHA Publishing Co., Ltd.
English publishing rights arranged directly with the author.

Book design: Andrew Pothecary (itsumo music)
Photography: Kobayashi Hiroshi (Spiral)
Technical supervisor: Yokoyama Manabu
Editorial assistance: Miyaguni Yukie

Printed in Japan
ISBN 978-4-86658-131-6
https://japanlibrary.jpic.or.jp/

Contents

Tundābun	4
Preface	10
Preface to the English Edition	
The Happiness and Sorrow of	
Okinawa	16
Foreword: Notes on Gozen honzō	18

Part One
The People and History behind
Ryukyu Cuisine

Meal served to the Chinese investiture
envoy at the accession of Shō Tai,
the last Ryukyu king ... 22
The Ryukyu king Shō Kō, instigator
of *Gozen honzō* ... 28
The Ryukyu cuisine of Ryukyu
aristocrat Baron Shō Jun ... 32

Part Two
Foodstuffs Used in Ryukyu Cuisine
Grains
Millet • *Mochimājin* ... 40
Peanuts • *Rakujishō* ... 42
Adzuki beans • *Akamame* ... 44
Mung beans • *Aomame* ... 46

Five Grains and Fermented Foods
Salt • *Shio* ... 48
Shōchū • *Shōchū* ... 50
Tofu ... 52
Four Main Ryukyuan Foods, Part 1
Island tofu ... 55

Dried tofu • *Rokujū* ... 58
Thin Japanese noodles • *Saumen* ... 59
Wheat gluten • *Fu* ... 60
Rice cake • *Mochi* ... 61
Wheat flour • *Muginoko* ... 62
• *Aburamochi* ... 62

Vegetables
Mustard greens • *Nā* ... 65
Fennel • *Mannen-uikyō* ... 66
Orange daylily • *Kansō* ... 67
Nigana ... 68
Japanese mugwort • *Futsuba* ... 70
Okinawan spinach • *Handama* ... 71
Mung bean sprouts • *Oyashi* ... 72
Peucedanum japonicum • *Bōfū* ... 73
Yellow carrot • *Kidaikon* ... 74
Island chilis • *Kōraigoshō* ... 75
Chinese onion • *Rakkyō* ... 76
Sweet potato • *Hantsun-imo* ... 78
Taro stems and leaves • *Imonoha* ... 78
Four Main Ryukyuan Foods, Part 2
Sweet potato: Potatoes with a history ... 79
Taro • *Ta-imo* ... 82

Gourds
Wax gourd • *Tōgai* ... 84
Bitter melon • *Gōya* ... 86
Sponge gourd • *Nāberā* ... 89
Nāberā dengaku (sponge gourd
coated with miso sauce) ... 90
Bottle gourd (calabash gourd) • *Tsuburu* ... 92
Okinawan yellow cucumber • *Mofu'uri* ... 92

Seaweed

Kombu • *Konbu* — 94
Four Main Ryukyuan Foods, Part 3
  Kombu: An exceptional trade item — 95
Seaweed • *Mō* — 99
Mozuku • *Sunori* — 100

Moss

Lichen • *Hatake-aosa* — 103

Livestock

Pork • *Buta-shishi* — 104
Minudaru (steamed pork) — 106
Leaf lard • *Buta-yu* — 108
Pork liver • *Buta-kimo* — 109
Pork lung • *Buta-fuku* — 110
Pork heart • *Buta-fukumame* — 110
Pork kidney • *Buta-mame* — 110
Pork stomach • *Buta-ohogai* — 111
Pork intestines • *Buta-wata* — 112
Pig trotters • *Buta-ashi* — 113
Pig blood • *Buta-ketsu* — 114
Four Main Ryukyuan Foods, Part 4
  Pigs: Eat everything except the oink — 115
Goat • *Hitsuji* — 118
Goat liver • *Hitsuji no kimo* — 118
Goat lung • *Hitsuji no fuku* — 118
Goat kidney • *Hitsuji no mame* — 119
Goat stomach • *Hitsuji no ohogai* — 119

Fish

Silver-stripe round herring • *Soreru* — 121
Porcupinefish • *Abasu* — 124
Broadclub cuttlefish • *Kubushime* — 125
Erabu eel • *Irabū unagi* — 126

Cooked Foods

Kamaboko steamed fish paste
  • *Kamaboku* — 127

Seafood

Gazami crab • *Gazame* — 128

Fruits

Lychee • *Leiki* — 131
Longan • *Ryugan* — 132
Shīkuwāshā • *Tachibana* — 133
Banana • *Baseo no mi* — 134
Sugarcane • *Ogi* — 135

Afterword — 138

Bibliography — 140

About the author — 142
About the translators — 142

Credits — 143

Preface

Traditional Cuisine of the Ryuku Islands: A History of Health and Healing is based on *Gozen honzō* (Edible plants of Ryukyu), a guidebook on Ryukyu diet therapy written by Tokashiki Pēchin Tsūkan, who was chief physician to the king of the Ryukyu Kingdom in the nineteenth century. Under the orders of King Shō Kō, Tsūkan went to China—then ruled by the Qing dynasty—and studied in Beijing. He finished the book in 1832, following his return from China. The copy I own is a 1964 reprinted edition that was edited by Tōma Kiyohiro and bound in traditional Japanese fashion. *Gozen honzō* comprises sixteen chapters—from chapter 1 on grains to chapter 16 on fruits and sweets—that describe the different types of traditional Ryukyu foods and how to combine them. Reading it, I get the feeling that it may be the source of the old Okinawan saying, "Food is *kusuimun* (medicine)."

Bitter melon (*gōya*), a well-known Okinawa vegetable, is mentioned in chapter 4. The vegetable is explained as follows: "Bitter melon is bitter and sweet, neutral, and nontoxic. Bitter melon removes pathogenic heat, reduces fatigue, cleanses the mind, and clears the vision. One can eat bitter melon every day during the summer months."

And the book deals with more than vegetables. Chapter 8 covers domestic animals such as chickens, ducks, and geese. Chapter 9 describes foods using wild game like pheasants, pigeons, and edible bird's nests. Chapter 10 tells us about water birds, such as herons and wild geese. Pork is a quintessential Okinawan food; pigs, together with goats and dogs, appear in chapter 11, which is on livestock. It explains the various parts of a pig—fat, liver, lungs, heart, kidneys, intestines, trotters, blood—with detailed descriptions of their medicinal effects and how to cook them.

✖

I picked up *Gozen honzō* about ten years ago at a used bookstore in Kyoto. The title didn't make it sound like an ancient book from the Ryukyus. The term *gozen* means "a tray on which the king's meal is served." A direct translation of *gozen honzō* would be "medicinal foods placed on a tray and served to the king." The book had a price of three dollars printed on its back cover, reminding me that Okinawa had been under US occupation at the time of its publication.

I came across *Gozen honzō* just as I was opening an Okinawan restaurant in Akasaka, Tokyo; I had been looking for ancient records and books about Ryukyu cuisine. The encounter with this book gave me the joy of discovery. It answered some questions, but evoked even more, and I decided that I had to find the answers.

The first big question was this: if herbs for food and medical treatment were already declining in popularity in Yamato (as Japan, then a separate country from the Ryukyus, was known in ancient times) at the beginning of the eighteenth century,[1] why was this book on them written in the Ryukyus in the middle of the nineteenth century? Another surprise was finding out that the information in the book was still in use today. Elders in Okinawa know a great deal about the efficacies and beneficial combinations of both common vegetables and wild plants. The source of their knowledge could very well have been the book that was in my hand.

About 230 years before Tsūkan wrote *Gozen honzō* (1604 or earlier), the *Compendium of Materia Medica*, by Li Shizhen, considered to be the most comprehensive book on Chinese medicine ever written, had been introduced to Yamato from China. Later, *Yamato honzō* (Medicinal herbs of Japan) was written in 1709 by Kaibara Ekiken, a Japanese Confucianist philosopher and botanist well known for his *Yōjōkun* (Book of life-nourishing principles). Since this book focused more on natural history than medicinal herbs, however, the concept of dietary therapy did not permeate the life of Japanese people as widely as it did in the Ryukyus.

In his research paper, "Ryukyu-koku shokuryōsho *Gozen honzō*" (The Ryukyuan food treatment book *Gozen honzō*), Yokoyama Manabu says, "*Gozen honzō* is written for cooks serving kings. It is both a book for explaining foods and a compilation of articles on food properties, effects, and compatibility. We can read about the ingredients in dishes prepared in the Ryukyu court. *Gozen honzō*, a guidebook on diet therapy (food combinations), is based upon the wide knowledge of medicine that Tokashiki Pēchin Tsūkan acquired in China."

When this guidebook was written, only Ryukyuans in the privileged classes were able to read and write. So why did its wisdom take root

---

1. Yokoyama Manabu, "Ryukyu-koku shokuryōsho *Gozen honzō*" [The Ryukyuan food treatment book *Gozen honzō*]. In *Seikatsu Bunka Kenkyūjo Nenpō* [Annual report of the Research Institute for Culture and Cultural History], vol. 1 (May 1987), published by the Research Institute for Culture and Cultural History, Notre Dame Seishin University.

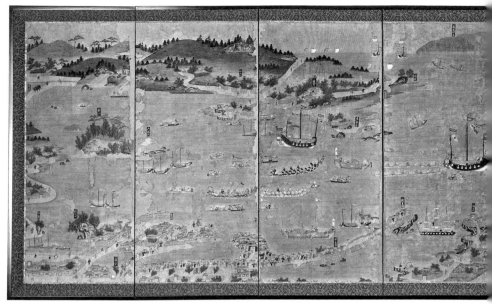

Nineteenth-century folding screen depicting Shuri and Naha Harbor. From the collection of the Okinawa Prefectural Museum and Art Museum. The harbor is busy with ships returning from taking tributes to China, ships belonging to the Satsuma domain, and ships from the West. Shuri Castle can be seen on the right-hand side.

in the lives of normal Ryukyu islanders? This question remained in my mind for a long time. In preparation for writing this cookbook, I asked Takara Kurayoshi of the University of the Ryukyus about it. According to him, there is a good chance that court doctors—whose work took them to various parts of the kingdom—taught common folk about medicinal foods.

During his reign, King Shō Kō dispatched many doctors to the Miyako and Yaeyama Islands. These doctors hired locals as assistants and taught them to administer simple treatments and dietary cures. "They are quick learners and competent," wrote one doctor about his islander helpers. In Ryukyu society, where the custom of healing by prayer was widespread, doctors' knowledge of diet therapy must have been valued and carefully passed on from person to person. Thus, teachings about food combinations and efficacies were disseminated among people who were illiterate and thus unable to read *Gozen honzō*.

Let me point out one more thing about this book. It has long been a "quiet" bestseller in Okinawa, where people find that it holds the "spirit

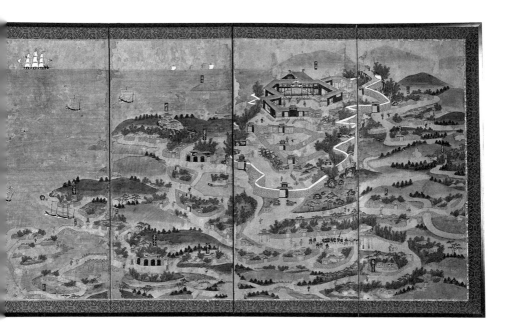

of food." Unlike books on herbs published in Yamato, *Gozen honzō* has two unique characteristics: it uses a Ryukyu dialect to describe the names of ingredients in kana characters, and it gives Ryukyuan recipes for some ingredients.

Why did Tsūkan do that? If he wrote the book only for cooks in the king's palace, he did not need to use the Ryukyu dialect; those cooks, called *hōchū*, were in a privileged class and therefore literate. My speculation is that the answer may well lie in the social conditions of Tsūkan's time. He was chief physician to the king, which meant he was a high-ranking official in the kingdom, so he must have traveled by horse as he went between the castle and the palace. He would have witnessed the lives of commoners along the way.

When *Gozen honzō* was published in 1832, Japan was nearing the end of the Edo period, and the Edo government had issued a sumptuary law in an effort to rebuild its finances. In the following year, one of the three major famines of the Edo period hit the country; it lasted until 1839. Floods and cold weather damaged Japan from the northeastern region to the island of Shikoku, and people were rioting in many cities. This tide of rebellion swept through the country, leading to the uprising led by Ōshio Heihachirō in 1837 and then to the start of the Tenpō Reforms in 1841.

The Ryukyus had suffered from typhoons and drought earlier, and

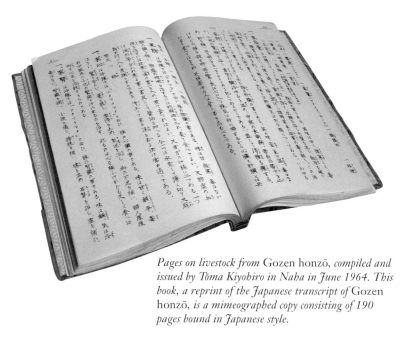

Pages on livestock from Gozen honzō, *compiled and issued by Tōma Kiyohiro in Naha in June 1964. This book, a reprint of the Japanese transcript of* Gozen honzō, *is a mimeographed copy consisting of 190 pages bound in Japanese style.*

were both suffering from natural catastrophes. Ryukyuans remained impoverished after Tsūkan's return home. The crop of sweet potatoes had failed, so people had to stave off hunger by eating sago palms. Legend has it that a thief once broke into King Shō Kō's palace in Urasoe-Gusukuma trying to steal one of the palms there. The thief was caught but not punished; instead, the king, taking into account the prevailing conditions, admonished him not to steal again and let him go. The famine was especially disastrous in 1832. A drought started in June, and people offered prayers for rain throughout the Ryukyus. In September, however, a terrible typhoon hit the islands, causing 2,455 people to die of starvation and 1,473 to die of an epidemic. According to records, the government opened up its warehouses to give aid to the people.

Gozen honzō was brought to the world in the midst of this unprecedented famine. Tsūkan saw the daily lives of commoners, so it is not difficult to imagine what thoughts crossed his mind while writing the manuscript.

Okinawans say "*Kusuinatan*" at the end of a meal. This means, "It was good medicine," and expresses gratitude to the person who made the dish. *Gozen honzō*, with its spiritual view of food as "good medicine," has been handed down from Ryukyuans to Okinawans, who continue to struggle to live their lives in a harsh natural environment.

Preface to the English Edition
The Happiness and Sorrow of Okinawa

Okinawa was once an independent country known as Ryukyu. The string of more than 140 islands of varying sizes describe an arc in the Pacific Ocean southwest of Japan, stretching from the southernmost tip of Kyushu all the way to Taiwan. These islands, known as the Ryukyu Arc, were once the Ryukyu Kingdom.

History shows that the Ryukyus became Okinawa after the end of the Edo period (1603-1868) when the Meiji government was established. In 1872, Japan annexed the Kingdom of Ryukyu as a *han*, or domain, before making it the prefecture of Okinawa in 1879, marking the end of the Ryukyu Kingdom.

After World War II, Okinawa was administered by the United States for twenty-seven years. The islands were of strategic geopolitical importance during the Cold War, referred to as keystones of the Pacific.

These several decades brought much hardship to Okinawa. During the years of the Ryukyu Kingdom, however, it flourished through trade with Taiwan, China and Korea, as well as other Asian countries, owing to its geographical location. A unique Ryukyu culture thrived in the midst of this age of interchange. Okinawa may be known today for its distinctive music and dancing, but there was much more than that. *Kasuri* weaving originated in India and spread through Southeast Asia, finally arriving in Ryukyu, which developed its own version of the textile art. The same happened with food. Pork came from China, and the meat continues to be loved in Okinawa where, famously, "everything gets eaten except the oink." In fact, pork had been an Okinawan staple for 400 years before the common folk on mainland Japan ever got a taste of it.

✄

This book, *Traditional Cuisine of the Ryukyu Islands: A History of Health and Healing*, is based on *Gozen honzō*, a book written in 1832 by Tokashiki Pēchin Tsūkan after he arrived home from China where he was sent by the king of the Ryukyus to learn about diet therapy.

The world in which the original work was written was one where people were constantly fighting famine and starvation; they needed information on food and nutrition just to stay alive. When I realized this fact, I felt as though I had made a brand new discovery about the ancient Ryukyu culture. How different dietary lifestyles are today, I thought, the way we insist on gourmet entrées and eat much more than is healthy. That was when I decided the timing was perfect to revisit the ancient teachings of *Gozen honzō*.

Elderly people in Okinawa still finish their meals by bowing and saying *kusuinatan* (that was good medicine) rather than the usual Japanese, *gochisōsama* (it was a feast). As I did research into and wrote about the lives of the ancient Ryukyuans, I became even more fascinated by them. I hope that readers who happened to pick up this book thinking it is a collection of recipes also enjoy the explanations of the cuisine and history of these southern islands that take them on a journey to Okinawa and the Ryukyu of days gone by.

Takagi Rin

Foreword: Notes on *Gozen honzō*

Gozen honzō, Edible Plants of Ryukyu, was written in the nineteenth century as a guide for the food served to the Ryukyu king. It explains the different foods, their properties and effects as well as incompatible combinations of ingredients. There is no other resource like this in existence. In *Traditional Cuisine of the Ryukyu Islands: A History of Health and Healing*, author Takagi Rin excerpts *Gozen honzō* and recreates the Ryukyu foods it describes. Photographs of the beautifully prepared dishes accompany the original recipes included in Takagi's work. The ingredients described herein are still a part of the Okinawan diet, eaten and widely appreciated as health foods with medicinal properties.

Gozen honzō was written by physician Tokashiki Pēchin Tsūkan, who was sent to China to study medicine. From ancient times the Chinese had sought to gain the immortality of Taoist ascetics. To this end, they studied natural objects, including plants, animals, and anything else considered to be curative, and compiled their knowledge into a field of study called herbalism. The term "herb" gives the impression of medicinal plants, but the original term actually meant "things based on herbs and minerals."

During the Liang dynasty in China, pharmacologist Tao Hongjing (456–536) created the foundation for herbalism by recording the names of 730 medicines. In 1596, Li Shizhen wrote *Compendium of Materia Medica*, a compilation of 1,871 names of natural things, and how they were used and categorized, all described in a unique way. Records show that *Materia Medica* reached Japan before 1609. It became not just the foundation for pharmacy, but also for Japanese natural history—in other words, all aspects of natural objects.

At about the same time, other books were published in China about dietary herbalism, studies of warnings about mixing certain foods together, the connections between foods and the different seasons, and the relationships between the five internal organs and the five tastes. The main purpose of the books was to teach people how to eat to keep their physical and mental capacities in optimal condition and health in order to live a long life. We can see that the properties of foods and dietary therapy became one field of herbalism when people began to think about the synergic effects of food and drugs as well as what foods should be avoided.

In the decades that followed, Japan also saw the publication of books on food. Some of these were *Yakusei nōdoku* (Medicinal effects and toxicity, 1608), *Nichiyō shokushō* (Daily diet, 1613), *Etsuho shokumotsu honzō* (Dietary herbalism reader, 1671), *Hōchū biyō wamyō honzō* (Japanese names for kitchen herbs, 1684), and *Honchō shokkan* (A material medica of the Edo period, 1697). *Shokumotsu honzō* (Food as materia medica, 1620) was brought from China, and many Japanese versions were printed. These books evolved into Japan's manuals on diet therapy, collectively known as *shokuryōyō-sho*.

Gozen honzō does not have close to the number of ingredients mentioned in *Shokumotsu honzō*, but focuses rather on foods that grew or were otherwise available in Ryukyu as well as some that could be imported there. *Gozen honzō* is valuable because it includes the names of many foods both in the Ryukyu dialect and Japanese, together with instructions on how to cook with them. Each section begins with the Ryukyu name in kana writing, followed by the Japanese name in kanji characters. We also get an idea of the unique diet of the islanders. For example, there are ten ways to serve pig including its blood, and five for cooking goat meat. Under sections on livestock and wild animals, we find only pigs, dogs, goats, cows, wild boars, and deer, which give us a good idea of animal life in Okinawa today. It is interesting to note that the version of *Compendium of Materia Medica* edited for use in Japan, as well as the other books on herbalism used in this country, made no mention of pork as an ingredient for food. At the time, there were religious restrictions on eating animals.

Other references in *Gozen honzō* include *Compendium of Materia Medica*, *Shokumotsu honzō*, *Wakan sansai-zue*, an Edo-period encyclopedia, and *Ryukyu kokushiryaku*, (Abridged history of the Ryukyu Kingdom). These resources add to our knowledge of local names for ingredients and how they were used in cooking. *Gozen honzō* thus gives an idea of how the book was compiled and about Okinawa food culture.

We assume that the foundation of the knowledge Tsūkan gained in China was *Compendium of Materia Medica*. To that he added the information contained in *Shokumotsu honzō*. He then incorporated food ingredients and combinations actually used in cooking in the Ryukyus, with the result being *Gozen honzō*. The book is not merely an accumulation of knowledge. The author's purpose was to provide a useful resource for daily life. Today, Tsūkan's achievement is of interest in the fields of linguistics, folklore, nutrition, and pharmacology.

Gozen honzō was a part of the Sakamaki and Hawley Collection of Frank Hawley (1906–1961), a world-renowned collector of precious books. Today it is in the archives of the University of Hawaii at Manoa Library, which houses many works related to the Ryukyu Kingdom. Three handwritten copies of *Gozen honzō* are still in existence, two of which were owned by Hawley—one bears the ownership stamp of "Nakagusuku Palace," and the other the stamp of "Mōsei Sueyoshi." The handwritings of these three transcribed copies are very similar, but contain some errors that the author would not have made if he were transcribing it himself. This led me to deduce the following theory: *Gozen honzō* was presented to the Ryukyu government by Tsūkan, where at least three copies of it were transcribed by somebody else. Subtle differences are evident among the three, such as kanji and kana transcriptions, indicating that the transcriber was most likely not a specialist in herbs and minerals.

Nevertheless, these are minor flaws; no other book has ever been written on the same subject, and *Gozen honzō* remains a work of great historical significance.

Yokoyama Manabu
Professor Emeritus, Notre Dame Seishin University

PART ONE

The People and History behind Ryukyu Cuisine

Meal served to the Chinese investiture envoy at the accession of Shō Tai, the last Ryukyu king

The Ryukyu Kingdom ended its five-hundred-year history when Japan entered the Meiji period. The kingdom was abolished by the Meiji government, which was trying—backed by military force—to rapidly modernize Japan. I will briefly describe the annexation of Ryukyu, an event not often mentioned in Japanese history.

In 1871, the Ryukyu royal government was placed under the jurisdiction of Kagoshima Prefecture, in accordance with the Meiji government's policy of abolishing feudal domains and establishing prefectures. In the following year, however, the Meiji government set up the Ryukyu Domain and named Shō Tai, the nineteenth king of Ryukyu, as its feudal lord. Seven years later in 1879, Matsuda Michiyuki,[1] a Meiji government official, announced the abolition of the Ryukyu Domain and established Okinawa Prefecture. That year, Nabeshima Naoyoshi took the post of prefectural governor, ending the rule of the Shō dynasty. The last Ryukyu king, Shō Tai, was given a *kazoku* (aristocracy) rank and ordered to relocate to Tokyo.

Although he lived in an age of turmoil, when Shō Tai took his throne, he welcomed the Chinese investiture envoy[2] with a five-tray meal comprising twenty dishes. This sumptuous feast, an assortment of delicacies from land and sea, was the last of its kind served to a Chinese mission by a Ryukyu ruler.

Banquet Menu for the Chinese Envoy
The handwritten script on page 23 shows the menu for a banquet presented to one member of the Chinese mission to the Ryukyu Kingdom in 1866. Some of the cooks working in the Shuri Castle

---

1. Matsuda Michiyuki (1839–82): A retainer of the feudal lord of Tottori Domain. After the Meiji Restoration, Matsuda worked as a government official in the Home Ministry of the Meiji government. In 1875, he was sent to Okinawa to annex the Ryukyu Kingdom. In 1879, after the annexation, he assumed the post of seventh governor of Tokyo.
2. When kings of vassal states to China (Ryukyu, Korea, Vietnam, etc.) acceded to the throne, the emperor of China, who had colonial power over them, sent imperial messages and addresses to the gods to recognize the kings as rulers. Investiture envoys came on ships called *ukwanshin* (crown ships). Twenty-two such Chinese missions came to the Ryukyus in the period from 1404 to 1866.

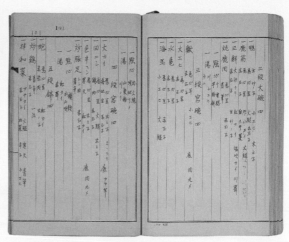

A handwritten copy of Genji gannen shina sappōshi rairyū shoki *(Visit of the Chinese investiture envoy to Ryukyu in Genji year 1). Courtesy of the University of the Ryukyus.*

kitchen had been trained in China, Kyoto, and Satsuma. They prepared a once-in-a-lifetime welcome meal, adding to Chinese dishes ingredients unavailable in China, such as horse crabs from the north and dugong meat from Ryukyu. Clearly, then, hospitality was an enormous expense for the Ryukyu government.

This banquet was held thirteen years prior to the end of the Ryukyu Kingdom. In June 1866, the mission comprising 434 officials arrived in Naha Harbor in two ships called *ukwanshin* (crown ships). The group stayed in the Ryukyus for 151 days, finally departing in November. The Chinese entourage was frequently entertained with such feasts, though the menus must have varied for officials of different ranks. Entertaining hundreds of people for five months was an extremely expensive endeavor. For example, to obtain enough pork, in addition to pigs from the main island, a total of 206 pigs had to be procured from the other islands that made up the kingdom: Ōshima and Yoron, and the Okino-Erabu Archipelago.

Financially distressed, the Ryukyu government had already borrowed money from Satsuma merchants and the Satsuma Domain. But those loans were not enough to keep up appearances as the royal government of a tributary state. *The New History of Ryukyu: Modern Era* (volume 1) published by the *Ryukyu Shimpo* newspaper company describes the situation this way:

The royal government in Shuri sent out an official notice throughout the kingdom to call for donations of money and crops. In response, *shizoku* privileged classes, local governors and officials such as *jitō-dai* and *utsuchi*, and even peasants donated money and crops. The government rewarded these peasants, giving them the title of *akahachimaki* or *chiku-doun*. In 1838, the government borrowed at least 145,000 *kanmon* (an old unit of currency; about 1.7 billion yen in today's currency) from about 130 people to pay for the king's investiture. Lenders were of course also rewarded with titles.

This demonstrates how excessively the Ryukyu government issued titles. Despite its financial difficulties, the kingdom continued to conduct the formalities required of a tributary state.

Readers may wonder what reasons the royal government had for straining its budget other than a desire to save face. In the early years of the relationship, profits from tributary trade with China exceeded expenses. The kingdom thrived on trade with Asian countries, enjoying the status of an affluent trade-based nation throughout the Great Ryukyu Age. But the tide shifted in 1609, when the Ryukyus were under the reign of the seventh king, Shō Nei. In that year, the Ryukyu Kingdom was invaded by the Satsuma clan. After the

Procession of the Investiture Envoy (shown in part). Eighteenth century. In the possession of the Okinawa Prefectural Museum and Art Museum. Ming-dynasty emperors allowed foreign states to trade with China only on the condition that they accept Chinese investiture and pay tribute to China. The Ryukyu Kingdom entered the tributary system of Ming China in 1372 and maintained a close relationship with China from then on. Investiture envoys from China are said to have comprised about 500 people. This drawing depicts a procession of envoys and officials traveling from their accommodations in Naha to Shuri Castle.

invasion, Shō Nei went to mainland Japan accompanied by the lord of Satsuma to meet Tokugawa Ieyasu in his retirement, and then to Edo for a formal audience with Shogun Tokugawa Hidetada. The Ryukyu king later swore oaths of loyalty to Satsuma, which allowed the kingdom to continue to exist and conduct trade under the clan's supervision. Despite its oath to Satsuma, the Ryukyu Kingdom had to continue its tributary relationship with China, the suzerain state, and maintain its appearance as a vassal state. This relationship was also convenient for the Satsuma clan, who wished to take advantage of the enormous profits of the Ryukyuan trade.

After the collapse of the Ryukyu Kingdom, the cooks in the king's kitchen who had made such splendid feasts disappeared into thin air.

Reproduction of the first of the five trays served to each guest at the 1866 banquet for the last investiture envoy. This tray has four large bowls, each one filled with ingredients considered luxurious.

Quail, matsutake *mushrooms, red boiled egg, green beans*

Sea cucumber, Chinese yam, chicken skin, Jinhua ham, dried bamboo shoot, red boiled egg

Horse crab, edible bird's nest, pine nuts, green beans, red boiled egg, Jinhua ham

Shark fin, shrimp, mushrooms, green beans, ham, chirimuji *noodles (made from wheat flour and egg yolk)*

The Ryukyu king Shō Kō, instigator of *Gozen honzō*

The Ryukyu dynasty, which can be divided into the first and second Shō dynasties, continued for about five hundred years. By comparison, the Tokugawa shogunate in Yamato only lasted about three centuries. The second Shō dynasty had nineteen kings, of which Shō Kō was the seventeenth. Shō Kō did not go down in history with a good reputation. Records show he had twenty-six children—nine boys and seventeen girls—by eleven women, including his queen, two other wives, and eight concubines. Eleven is the largest number of mothers of a single king's children in the history of the dynasty. The king is thus said to have given himself up to carnal pleasures, taking little responsibility for the administration of the kingdom.

As mentioned in the preface, Tokashiki Pēchin Tsūkan, the author of *Gozen honzō*, went to China twice under the orders of King Shō Kō. In his time, a journey to China was a life-risking endeavor. Even today, "to take a trip to China" in the Okinawan dialect means "to go on one's last journey." Did Tsūkan go to China twice for the sake of a king who indulged in the pleasures of the flesh and ignored his duty as ruler?

The facts show that in 1825 the Ryukyu Islands suffered from a great famine. Moreover, foreign ships were arriving one after another, demanding interviews with the king and requesting that he open up the kingdom. (The late-eighteenth-century collection "Drawings of World Ship Ensigns" by Yamaguchi Suio shows the flags of merchant ships from numerous foreign countries, including England and the Netherlands.) On the mainland, the Tokugawa shogunate had to cope with the same sort of situation, and responded by promulgating the Edict to Repel Foreign Vessels. Beset with troubles both at home and abroad, in 1827, Shō Kō built a palace in Gusukuma, Urasoe City, and left Shuri Castle with his wives and concubines, abandoning his duties to the kingdom in times of hardship. Did King Shō Kō really just lose himself in lust for women?

We get a different impression of the king in the context of Tsūkan's *Gozen honzō*. Shō Kō was enthroned in 1804 at the age of eighteen. Soon after his accession to the throne, the king wrote a poem: *If I am not attentive, please punish me alone and save the people from suffering*. The poem seems to express the pure aspirations of the young king.

The seventeenth king of the second Shō dynasty, Shō Kō (r. 1804–1834). This is a monochrome photo of an ogoe, *or posthumous portrait, which was a custom that developed in Ryukyu. The original painting was lost during Word War II. Photograph by Kamakura Yoshitarō. In possession of the Okinawa Prefectural University of Arts.*

The Ryukyus had long suffered hardships caused by frequent maritime accidents and poverty in rural communities. Shō Kō later wrote another poem in which he deplored the social conditions of the time, lamenting that some officials and privileged classes were filling their own pockets and building storehouses while the royal family and citizens were leading frugal lives. These poems make me see the king in a different light. Shō Kō tried to carry out political reform by getting rid of his chief retainers. However, he was apparently no match for the cunning vassals, and failed in his attempts. He was gradually reduced to being a king in name only, pushed to the side by his own vassals.

✳

In 1828, the year following his departure from Shuri Castle, Shō Kō abdicated in favor of his son Shō Iku, according to *Chūzan seifu* (Genealogy of Chūzan), an official history of the Ryukyu Kingdom. At this time, Shō Kō was only forty-two years old; Shō Iku was a tender youth of just sixteen. According to *Tōtei zuihitsu* (Tōtei's miscellaneous writings), an account written by the son of a royal aide after the king's death, Shō Kō was forced to abdicate due to a

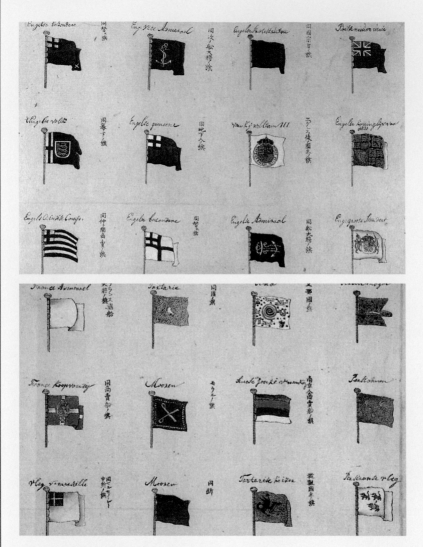

"Drawings of World Ship Ensigns" shows flags of merchant ships from many foreign countries. From the catalog "Rekishi o hiraku: Ryukyu bunka hihō ten" [Looking into history: The secret treasures of Ryukyu culture], Seventieth anniversary of the Naha municipal government, 1991.

nervous breakdown. Such an illness, however, is frequently used throughout history to explain the abdication of kings who were caught up in power struggles. Tsūkan came back from his second trip to China in 1827, the year that Shō Kō left Shuri Castle. If Tsūkan had been sent to China to find a cure for the king's illness, or "nervous breakdown," the doctor returned too late to cure him when he was still on the throne.

Tsūkan wrote *Gozen honzō* in 1832, when Shō Kō had already retired. It was also the year when a great famine devastated the Ryukyus. At that time, the retired Shō Kō made a vegetable garden at his palace in Gusukuma and grew bottle gourds, Japanese sago palms, and other vegetables. The gourds harvested there were sold on the market as "master's gourds." Cultivation of sago palms as an emergency food had been promoted by the royal government, but Shō Kō's involvement in this promotion is unknown.

In 1834, two years after the publication of *Gozen honzō*, legend has it that Shō Kō threw himself into the sea with a great cry and drowned. *Tōtei zuihitsu* says the king jumped into the water while he was out boating. He must have been accompanied by attendants. I wonder if they did all they could to rescue him. The sudden death of Shō Kō seems unnatural, especially when I think of his interest in dietary medicine and his attempt to make a vegetable garden during a time of famine.

We have no clue as to what kind of relationship Shō Kō and Tsūkan had as master and servant. But one thing seems to be certain: *Gozen honzō* would not have existed if the king had not sent the young doctor to China or had had no interest in the medicinal properties of foods. After Shō Kō's death, Tsūkan served the eighteenth king, Shō Iku. The physician passed away in 1846 at the age of fifty-three.

Tsūkan left us this book on medicinal foods. Its value seems to be growing in the modern age, when so much of the world is faced with a lack of food.

The Ryukyu cuisine of Ryukyu aristocrat Baron Shō Jun

The phrase "Life itself is a treasure" represents the spirit of Okinawa. This phrase comes from the poem that Shō Tai, the last king of the Ryukyus, is said to have read when he left Shuri Castle for the last time. The poem goes: "The time for wars is ending. The time for peace is not far away. Do not despair. Life itself is a treasure."

The words in this poem resound with the people of Okinawa when they recall their horrific experiences during the Battle of Okinawa in World War II. The last sentence in particular has been used widely in Okinawan peace movements.

�֎

Shō Jun, the fourth son of King Shō Tai, was called Prince Matsuyama, as his residence was in the Matsuyama Palace in Shuri. He was seven years old when the king abandoned Shuri Castle in 1879. A collection of Shō Jun's writings published posthumously recount his memories of that time:

> An old man with a white beard waited upon my father (Shō Tai) in his living room. I watched the old man talking loudly about something. Oddly, I remember seeing his long white beard quiver on his chest each time he spoke. I wonder when we moved from Shuri Castle to Nakagusuku Odon (Palace). Maybe it was the night of March 8, because the surrender was on March 9. I remember the bustle and confusion of people and a bonfire bright against the dark sky. I entered the palace carried on the back of my nanny.[3]

This passage conveys the unusual atmosphere of the night. Sometime later, Matsuda Michiyuki, clad in Western clothes, stood in front of the alcove of the South Palace in Shuri Castle. In his ringing voice, Matsuda delivered the official notice of the abolition of feudal domains and the establishment of prefectures.

---

3. *Matsuyama ōji Shō Jun ikō* [Writings by Prince Matsuyama Shō Jun] compiled by Yamazato Eikichi (Shō Jun Manuscripts Publishing Committee, 1969).

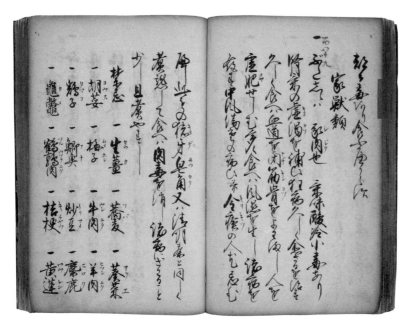

One of the existing copies of Gozen honzō, *formerly owned by Frank Hawley. From the Sakamaki and Hawley Collection in the University of Hawaii at Manoa Library. Shown here are the pages on livestock. The book was written in ink on 137 leaves of* washi *paper bound in Japanese style. The ownership stamp of "Nakagusuku Odon" (Nakagusuku Palace) indicates that the book belonged to the Ryukyu Kingdom government.*

a devastating famine had occurred from 1820 to 1824. This famine is recorded in the *Kyūyō*, an official history of the Ryukyu Kingdom compiled by the royal government. The record says, "There are a great many beggars and starving people." And famine was not the only worry of the government. Dutchmen and Englishmen were arriving in ships and requesting audiences with the king. The West was just beginning to pay attention to the Far East.

Tokashiki Pēchin Tsūkan was born in 1794 in Shuri, according to his genealogical record. His accomplishments as a doctor led King Shō Kō to send him to study in Beijing at the age of twenty-four. When Tsūkan came back to Japan three years later in May 1820, the famine was devastating the entire Ryukyu Kingdom. He was appointed physician to the king, and was sent to China again in September 1824 to find a cure for the king's illness. When he returned home safely in April 1827, Tsūkan was thirty-four years old.

This was a time of crisis for Yamato and the Ryukyu Kingdom, which

Baron Shō Jun (1873–1945) in his later years in the Kōrei Sanbō teahouse. He was known as an entrepreneur and a man of culture who was knowledgeable about Chinese poetry, Ryukyuan verses, artworks, and antiques. Courtesy of Heibonsha Publishing.

Shō Jun went to Tokyo in 1885, when he was thirteen. Shō Tai, who had been made a marquis, lived in a house in Kudan Sakaue, Tokyo. Shō Jun stayed with his father until the age of fifteen, spending two years of his impressionable youth in the milieu of the new Meiji period. After returning to Okinawa with his second-oldest brother Shō In, Shō Jun founded the *Ryukyu Shimpo* newspaper at the age of twenty-one. The young days of this princely man are depicted in *Chūgaku jidai no omoide* (Memoir of junior-high-school days) by Iha Fuyū, a pioneer of Okinawan studies. "Prince Matsuyama, the central figure (in the founding of the *Ryukyu Shimpo*), was twenty-two years old [sic] that year. His hair was twisted on top of his head and held with a gold hairpin. He always travelled between Shuri and Naha, riding a Yamato horse."

Shō Jun was a well-read person with a profound knowledge of artworks and antiques. He established a close relationship with painter Tomioka Tessai, who called him the "prince of Okinawa." The prince frequently visited the painter's studio in Kyoto and owned a number of his paintings and letters. It is a great pity that these works were scattered and lost during the war. Shō Jun was made a baron at the age of twenty-four and was elected to the House of Peers of the Imperial Diet at thirty-two. While finding much pleasure in his hobbies, he kept his focus on the future of Okinawa and acted as a business leader. After resigning his government post in 1915, Shō Jun played a major role in promoting Okinawa's economy. He was engaged in the reclamation of 16,500 square meters of ocean in the old Naha district. In Tobaru, Shuri, he developed an experimental plantation for growing subtropical fruit trees. He pioneered pineapple cultivation in Okinawa.

⚒

As a multitalented man representing Okinawa, Shō Jun received a number of visitors from the mainland, including artists and scholars. At the end of 1938, art critic and philosopher Yanagi Muneyoshi visited Okinawa with thirty-odd scholars and artists. The Naha city government and the *Ryukyu Shimpo* held large receptions for the group at restaurants in Naha. Hearing that they had been disappointed with Ryukyu cuisine, Shō Jun said, "I'll treat the group to delicious Ryukyu dishes at my house, but not everyone—only fifteen of them. I'll leave the selection to Mr. Yanagi." He then invited the chosen fifteen to his house in Shuri. Meals served at the home of epicurean Shō Jun were reputed to be the best in Okinawa. Unfortunately, we don't have a menu of the dinner given to the group, but the way Shō Jun acted as host is described by Yamazato Eikichi, the editor of his manuscripts. In the essay titled "Shō Jun danshaku to watashi" (Baron Shō Jun and me), Yamazato wrote,

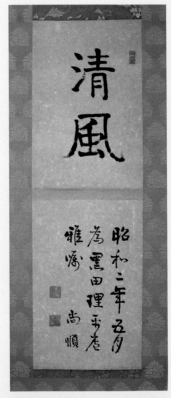

Calligraphy "Cool Breeze" by Baron Shō Jun, owned by the Shō family.

> Shō Jun entertained guests in a certain way that never changed much. First, guests were led to a sixteen-mat drawing room. They were served tea and sweets. After a while, Shō Jun showed up in full dress of *haori* (traditional jacket) and *hakama* (traditional skirt-like pants). He never received his guests dressed casually.

Baron Shō Jun's feast reproduced on a cabriole-leg tray, based on descriptions in Matsuyama ōji Shō Jun ikō *(Writings by Prince Matsuyama Shō Jun). Long plate in front (from right to left): boiled egg, dried sea cucumber, roasted Japanese quail,* minudaru *(steamed pork with sesame), green* kamaboko *steamed fish paste. Small plates from right:* duruwakashī *(cooked taro),* chimu-machi *pork liver,* mimigā *(pig ear) sashimi.*

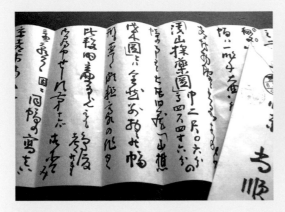

Handwritten letter by Baron Shō Jun, addressed to a friend in Kyoto. The kanji characters are brushed in a flowing hand. Courtesy of Kanpōdō Fine Arts.

The book goes on to describe how, after making small talk, the baron led his guests to the garden. He was proud of the potted melon vines that grew in the greenhouse. The plants reputedly produced melons all year round. He then led the group to the Kōrei Sanbō teahouse. By the time they returned to the drawing room, the table had been set, with a rare vintage of *awamori* (distilled rice liquor), one of Shō Jun's proudest possessions, waiting for them.

A year prior to the Yanagi group's visit to Okinawa, painter Fujita Tsuguharu had returned home from France and travelled around Okinawa. He wrote about a night at Shō Jun's house in his essay titled "Shuri no Shō Jun danshaku" (Baron Shō Jun in Shuri).

The banquet started. The hundred-year-old *awamori* was as light as vintage French wine. Carrot, roasted tofu, shrimp, seaweed, bamboo shoots, and soymilk skin were served in red Ryukyu-lacquered bowls adorned with the Shō family's emblem of three comma-shaped figures in a circle. Served next were sea cucumber and egg yolk, *kamaboko* made with pig entrails, and a dish of shrimp and wood-ear mushroom tempura. We relished fifty-year-old plum liqueur [note: this may have been *awamori*]. . . . Discussion of literature, music, dance, and paintings continued the entire time we dined, with both topics and culinary delights offered in unending succession. When we returned from his house, the crescent of the moon had already set beneath the sea horizon. I walked on a dark graveled path surrounded by glimmering fireflies. The hospitality I received in the Ryukyus this night was one of the unforgettable memories of my life.

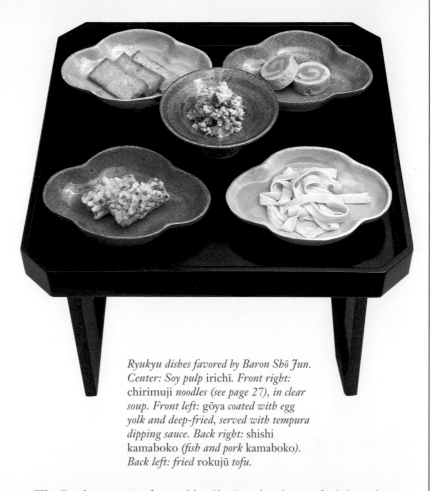

Ryukyu dishes favored by Barон Shō Jun.
Center: Soy pulp irichī. *Front right:*
chirimuji *noodles (see page 27), in clear*
soup. Front left: gōya *coated with egg*
yolk and deep-fried, served with tempura
dipping sauce. Back right: shishi
kamaboko *(fish and pork* kamaboko*).*
Back left: fried rokujū *tofu.*

The Ryukyu cuisine favored by Shō Jun deeply satisfied the palates
and hearts of his connoisseur guests. The feasts given by the baron,
who had encountered all kinds of gourmet foods in Kyoto and
Tokyo, are said to have placed more emphasis on flavor than on the
authenticity of traditional Okinawa cuisine.

The life of epicure Shō Jun ended in June 1945, when he was
seventy-three. He died of starvation in a cave in southern Okinawa,
where he had evacuated with troops near the end of World War II.
There was neither water nor food in the cave. This noble man was
said to have wetted his mouth by dipping mugwort in the muddy
water that filled holes left by bullets.

PART TWO

Foodstuffs Used in Ryukyu Cuisine

The categorization and section titles
are based on *Gozen honzō*.

Notes on the text that follows:

All the entries on foods are in *Gozen honzō* by Tokashiki
Pēchin Tsūkan.

The excerpts at the beginning of each entry are from a
reprint of *Gozen honzō* compiled and issued by Tōma Kiyohiro
(1964) and the article "Ryukyukoku shokuryōsho *Gozen honzō*"
[The Ryukyuan food treatment book *Gozen honzō*] written by
Yokoyama Manabu, which appeared in *Seikatsu bunka kenkyūjo
nenpō* [Annual report of the Research Institute for Culture and
Cultural History] vol. 1 (May 1987) and vol. 2 (November
1988) published by the Research Institute for Culture and
Cultural History at Notre Dame Seishin University.

The excerpts mention five tastes: sweet, pungent, salty, sour,
and bitter. The classifications of cold (very cold), cool, neutral,
warm, and hot (very hot) indicate the cooling or warming
effects of foods on the body. Food is neutral when it does not
make the body noticeably cold, cool, warm, or hot.

Millet · *Mochimājin*

Mochimājin is *Panicum miliaceum*, a type of millet. It is sweet, warms the body, and is nontoxic.

Millet increases qi energy and strengthens digestive organs. Consuming too much generates heat and sedates the five internal organs so that one sleeps well. Millet relaxes muscles and bones and weakens the pulse. Eating in excess will render children unable to walk for a long time. Sick people and small children should avoid eating millet.

Incompatible foods: Whorled mallow, beef

Millet, called *mochimājin* or *mochikibi* in Okinawa, originated in India. In China, it is considered one of the five staple grains.[1] These days, people may be more familiar with millet husks used to make handicrafts.

Millet dumplings, which are often mentioned in Japanese folklore, were a delicacy in olden times. People in Okinawa still eat millet, but not as dumplings. In the Yaeyama region (Ishigaki and Iriomote Islands), the main festival dish, *iiyachi*, is made by cooking sticky rice with the five grains. This dish is also mentioned in ancient books. It is offered to the *onarigami* holy women (based on the ancient belief that female siblings provide spiritual protection for their brothers) during the Seeding Festival, which is held at the time of sowing to pray for a rich harvest.

Millet, or mochikibi

---

1. The five grains are rice, wheat or barley, foxtail millet, white millet, and soybeans.

Iiyachi

★ Ingredients
Sticky rice, five grains, Japanese
banana leaves or shell ginger leaves
★ Directions
Cook the sticky rice together
with the five grains. Mash the
combination into a coarse paste.
Then form it into bars and wrap
in Japanese banana leaves or shell
ginger leaves. Steam.

Peanuts
• *Rakujishō*

**Rakujishō, or peanuts (*Arachis hypogaea*), are spicy
and sweet; they smell good and
are nontoxic.**
Peanuts moisten the lungs,
strengthen the spleen, and treat a
dry cough. They should not be eaten
by people suffering from wounds,
smallpox, or measles.

Said to originate in the Andes of
Bolivia, peanuts were brought
over to Japan at the beginning of
the eighteenth century via India
and China.

They are known by many
names in Japan: "China beans,"
"Nanking beans," "foreigners'
beans," and "Kantō beans." Since
they came from China, peanuts
could have been called "China
beans" in Okinawa, but locals call
them "*jīmami*," or "ground nuts."
We don't know how long that
name has been used.

Okinawa is hit every year by
severe typhoons that utterly
destroy everything growing on
the land, but sweet potatoes
and peanuts remain intact
underground. Peanuts were a
precious food source in the old
days, and as they became more
common, locals began to call
them *jīmami*; that is, nuts that
grow in the earth.

*Peanuts,
or* jīmami

Jīmami dōfu (peanut-tofu squares)

★ **Ingredients**

For the tofu: raw peanuts, potato starch or Yoshino kudzu starch, tapioca starch (optional).
For garnish: grated ginger. Sauce made of equal parts dashi stock, soy sauce, and mirin.

★ **Directions**

Soak the raw peanuts in water overnight and then remove the papery skin. Combine
the peanuts with half their amount of water (by volume) in a mortar and grind them
together. Wrap the ground peanuts in cheesecloth and squeeze the liquid into a
saucepan, discarding the solids. Add potato starch or Yoshino kudzu starch in half
the amount of the discarded peanut solids and bring to a boil. Add tapioca powder,
if available, to thicken further. Stir the liquid continuously with a wooden spoon.
When it becomes clear and thick, remove from heat and pour into a mold. Let it
cool, then remove the tofu from the mold. Cut into desired serving portions and top
each portion with grated ginger and sauce.

Adzuki beans ·*Akamame*

Akamame are *Vigna (Phaseolus) angularis* or adzuki beans. They are sweet and sour, neutral, and nontoxic.

Adzuki beans treat edema, abscesses, and chills. They halt diarrhea and acid reflux, act as a diuretic, and relieve abdominal bloating and thirst. They activate qi energy, improve the spleen and stomach, and increase appetite. The broth of cooked adzuki beans detoxifies alcohol. Simmer with carp and eat as a treatment for edema, beriberi, and rheumatism.

The flowers of the adzuki plant relieve the headache and thirst of a hangover; they are the best medicine for detoxifying alcohol. The flowers may be picked in July and dried in the shade; they can then be brewed like tea or added to soup.

Adzuki beans

This is an excerpt of the full list of efficacies from *Gozen honzō*, which says adzuki beans are good for rheumatism, and even details how the flowers should be picked in July to cure a hangover.

Elsewhere in Japan, adzuki beans are usually boiled and mashed into a paste to make adzuki jam or sweet bean-paste confections. In tropical regions, however, these sweets spoil quickly, so Okinawans have traditionally cooked adzuki beans and used them whole.

On the 15th of August according to the lunar calendar—the day called *junguyā*—Okinawans make an offering of *fuchagi* (mochi rice cakes topped with sweetened adzuki beans). They offer the *fuchagi* to the moon and to Hinukan, the god of fire, as well as on the family Buddhist altar, praying for the well-being of their families.

Fuchagi (mochi with sweet beans)

★ Ingredients
Mochiko sweet rice flour, adzuki beans, sugar
★ Directions
On the mainland of Japan, mochi is made by pounding steamed rice, but in Okinawa, as in China, sweet rice flour is mixed with water to make a dough. Knead the rice-flour dough until it is as soft as an earlobe and shape into small balls, sprinkling with starch powder to prevent them from sticking together. Cover the mochi with cooked and sweetened adzuki beans.

Mung beans • *Aomame*

Mung beans, or aomame

Aomame, or mung beans (*Vigna radiata*), are sweet, have a cooling effect, and are nontoxic.

Mung beans get rid of swelling, reduce heat, make qi energy flow downward, increase stamina, harmonize the five internal organs, calm the mind, enhance flow of the meridians, relieve symptoms of light colds, and moisturize the skin. Mung beans are recommended as part of a regular diet. Broth made of the beans assuages thirst, treats smallpox, relieves swelling, cures edema, halts chills and diarrhea, and promotes urination.

As a medicinal treatment, mung beans remove toxicity in meat taken from sick oxen or horses, and are an antidote for metal and mineral poisoning. Using a bag filled with mung beans as a pillow relieves headaches, improves eyesight, and alleviates acid reflux.

Incompatible foods: pine nuts, vinegared carp

Mung beans are easy to sprout, and mung bean sprouts are used in many dishes (see page 72). Glass noodles are made by boiling mung bean starch in water, spreading the resulting paste over a sheet, and cutting it into thin noodles. Mung beans are also used as feed for cows and horses.

One of the described qualities of mung beans is that they remove toxicity from the meat of sick oxen or horses and neutralize metal and mineral poisoning. This description comes from the *Compendium of Materia Medica*, a volume written by the Chinese herbologist Li Shizhen during the Ming dynasty of China. That book, however, made no mention of a mung bean "pillow," which seems to be an idea added by Tsūkan when he wrote *Gozen honzō*. In Okinawa, mung beans are used not only to produce sprouts, but also to make mung bean jelly and sweet mung bean soup.

Amagashi (sweet mung bean soup)

★ Ingredients
Mung beans, white or brown sugar, purple *mochiko* sweet rice flour (use regular *mochiko* if purple is not available)

★ Directions
Soak the mung beans in water overnight. The next day, drain and rinse them, then bring to a boil in plenty of water. Cook over medium heat for 30 to 40 minutes, skimming off the scum that rises to the surface. If the heat is too high, the beans will burst open, so watch them carefully. Add rolled barley if desired. When the beans are soft, add sugar or fruit sugar a little at a time to taste. Stir in a pinch of salt at the end. To make the mochi dumplings, add water to the sweet rice flour and knead the dough until it is about as soft as an earlobe. Shape into small balls and add them to boiling water. When the dumplings float to the surface, transfer to a cold-water bath to cool, then drain. Serve the mung bean soup in a bowl with a few dumplings on top.

Aomame yōkan (mung bean jelly) *On opposite page*

★ Ingredients
Mung beans, *kanten* (agar) (5 to 7 grams for every 500 grams of mung beans), sugar (half the amount of the mung beans)

★ Directions
Soak the mung beans and *kanten* (agar) separately in water overnight. Drain the beans well. Add the sugar and just enough water to cover. Bring to a boil over medium heat and simmer for 30 to 40 minutes. (Keep an eye on the heat; if it is too high, the mung beans will burst.) When the beans become soft enough, remove from heat and put through a strainer or ricer to make a paste. Drain the *kanten*, add a small quantity of fresh water, and stir until the agar dissolves completely. Gradually stir the bean paste into the agar liquid, then pour it into a mold to set.

Salt • *Shio*

Shio is sweet and salty, makes the body cold, and is nontoxic.
The Ryukyuan word for salt is *māsu*. Salt removes toxins, purifies qi energy, and expels lung diseases. Scrub your teeth with salt and water every morning; spit it out and use it to rinse your eyes, and you will be able to read small print even at night. Consuming too much salt darkens the skin, decreases muscle power, and causes thirst. Salt should be avoided by people suffering from edema, diabetes, or gonorrhea.

Shimamāsu (salt)

"Brush your teeth with salt and water . . . spit it out and use it to rinse your eyes." This instruction makes us think of a time when salt was precious. Surrounded by beautiful seas, Okinawa is now famous for its production of natural salt. In the Ryukyu period, however, salt was purchased from merchants in Satsuma, a feudal domain of southern Kyushu.

Satsuma's salt-making technique was brought to Ryukyu in 1694, and salt making started in a tidal wetland near a harbor in Naha. Locals were unable to produce as much as they needed, however. The Ryukyu government ordered the Yaeyama islanders to produce salt, but they refused, believing that boiling seawater would bring disaster. One theory explaining this belief holds that people did not like cutting down trees as fuel for boiling seawater.

Gurukun boiled in *māsu* salt water

★ Ingredients

Gurukun banana fish (*Pterocaesio digramma*),
kombu broth, salt, bonito flakes, fennel fronds

★ Directions

This is a dish to make on the beach. The fish
is boiled in broth seasoned only with salt and
bonito flakes. The fennel is added to remove
the fish smell.

Shōchū · *Shōchū*

Shōchū is a Japanese spirit distilled from sweet potatoes, rice, or wheat. It is pungent and sweet, hot, and extremely toxic.

Shōchū *is also called firewater. A small amount of* shōchū *reduces dampness, gets rid of chills, alleviates anger, halts thoracic choking, removes phlegm and rheum, and stops cold pains. However, drinking too much causes a flush, headache, and acid reflux, and reduces stamina. Taking either a cold or hot bath after drinking* shōchū *should be avoided because it can lead to sudden death.*

Incompatible foods: Ginger, garlic

Tōfuyō *fermented tofu served on a plate alongside* awamori; *sake drinking set made by Ōmine Jissei*

Gozen honzō introduces four alcoholic beverages—*shōchū*, sake, *shōchū* lees, and *amazake*, a sweet drink made overnight from fermented rice—but there is no mention of *awamori*. *Awamori* was brought to Ryukyu from Siam (now Thailand). It was a new type of liquor made from long-grained *indica* rice fermented with *Aspergillus luchuensis* and then distilled.

The term *awamori* was used for the first time in history in 1671, when it appeared on the list of gifts presented to the shogun. This term is said to have been used to distinguish between *shōchū* from Ryukyu and *shōchū* from Satsuma. In later years, Arai Hakuseki described the distillation method for *awamori*—not *shōchū*—in his book *Nantōshi* (History of the southern islands). However, in the late Edo period when *Gozen honzō* was written, the term *awamori* was not yet in common use in the Ryukyu Islands.

Tōfuyō (fermented tofu)

★ Ingredients
Rice *kōji*, *awamori*, coarse-grained Okinawan tofu, salt, *ang-khak* red rice mold
Note: *Kōji* rice is sake rice inoculated with spores of *Aspergillus oryzae*. *Ang-khak*, known in China as "red yeast rice," is a cultivated mold used in the production of certain fermented foods.

★ Directions
Soak the rice *kōji* in *awamori* and let it ferment for about ten days. Drain the tofu and cut into small cubes. Sprinkle with salt and let the tofu dry for several days. After drying, rinse the salt off with additional *awamori*. Grind the fermented rice *kōji* and a small amount of *ang-khak* into a paste in a mortar. Coat the dried tofu in this paste and allow to stand in a covered container, in a cool, draft-free place, for three to six months.

The Yokoyama edition of *Gozen honzō* includes *tōfuyō* in its own section, separate from tofu. The author describes it this way: "*Tōfuyō* is an appealing food that is good for the stomach. It is delightful to eat and good for all kinds of illnesses." *Tōfuyō* is said to have evolved in Ryukyu from Chinese fermented bean curd.

Tofu

Tofu is sweet and salty. It has a cooling effect on the body, and is slightly toxic.
Tofu relaxes the internal organs, increases qi energy, harmonizes the spleen and stomach, and relieves bloating. It cleans the large intestines, lowers heat, and reduces blood stagnation.

Yushi-dōfu soup uses tofu in its fluffy state before it is compressed into a cake. Spoon the soft *yushi-dōfu* into a bowl, add hot broth, and sprinkle on condiments such as chopped scallions and a few drops of *kōrēgusu* (chilis preserved in *awamori*) before serving.

Yushi-dōfu can be compressed into Okinawan tofu. Pour *yushi-dōfu* into a mold lined with cheesecloth or muslin, cover, and place a weight on top. Yanagita Kunio, a Japanese scholar and folklorist, refers in an essay to "tofu in the shape of a peach." This may have been made by placing *yushi-dōfu* in a bag and compressing it into a round shape.

Yushi-dōfu

Ukara irichī (simmered *okara* soy pulp)

★ **Ingredients**

Pork, carrot, *kamaboko* steamed fish paste, shiitake mushrooms, green peas, *ukara* soy pulp, pork broth. Adding a wood-ear mushroom will make the dish even tastier.

★ **Directions**

Ukara refers to *okara*, or soy pulp. Dice boiled pork or end pieces. Cut the carrot, *kamaboko*, and shiitake mushrooms in the same manner. Sauté the meat and vegetables in oil. Stir in the *ukara* and then add the pork broth. When the *ukara* is well coated, season with sugar, soy sauce, and salt. If pork broth is not available, use dashi stock made of shaved dried bonito (*katsuobushi*) and kombu.

Tofu-coated sashimi

★ **Ingredients**

Light-fleshed fish (such as sea bass, snapper or tilapia), kombu seaweed, tofu

★ **Directions**

The photo shows *akamachi* (queen snapper), a red-skinned fish found in Okinawa.

Fillet the fish and remove the skin. Sandwich it between two sheets of kombu and let stand for half a day. Cut the fillet into slices as desired. Drain the tofu and dry-roast it in a pan, stirring with a wooden spoon. When tofu is dry and crumbly, sprinkle it around the fish.

Island tofu

Island tofu, loved by both aristocrats and commoners,
is as strong and sturdy as a wandering samurai.

In 1920, ninety years after Tsūkan wrote *Gozen honzō*, folklorist Yanagita Kunio set out on his journey to explore Okinawa, a trip he had long wanted to make. His aim was to find out about the lives and history of ordinary Okinawans, who had been long ignored, by studying records of legends and other documents. Yanagita spent almost a month travelling around Okinawa that winter, and as a result became a pioneer in the study of Okinawan folklore.

Yanagita wrote down his experiences in *Kainan shōki* (Notes on the Southern Sea), which contains the section titled "A Story of Tofu." He depicted the "tofu scenery" that he saw as he walked from Shuri to Naha, and then along a seaside road stretching to Nago in the northern part of the island.

Walking down the Nago road from Irijuku, one sees so many households making and selling tofu that sellers seem to outnumber buyers. Each house has a stone fence in the front yard, shaded by its inevitable banyan tree at one end. Hung from a branch or placed on a post is an old beer case outfitted with a glass plate containing a few pieces of tofu. This setup is an "unattended shop." . . . In shops like this bean curds are squeezed, boiled, and then molded in a box with a pressing lid. Locals seem to put the box and the lid together in a pot of boiling water. The lid, shaped like a *geta* sandal, leaves the black marks of its teeth on the tofu. I also see tofu in the shape of a large peach, resembling the balls of soy pulp sold in mainland Japan. Tofu is cut into four or eight pieces and offered for sale. It is as strong and sturdy as a wandering samurai. If the delicately fragile silken tofu of the big city were faced with its country cousin, it would certainly cover its face in embarrassment.

On the way from Shuri to Naha, Yanagita met women carrying buckets on their heads who were heading for a saltworks at the harbor to acquire *nigari*, a liquid extracted from seawater that is used to make tofu coagulate. His depiction of the encounter makes us imagine genre pictures of the time.

In his youth, Yanagita met Shimazaki Tōson and other novelists who taught him about naturalist literature. Reading such works made Yanagita interested in social issues, and he intended to study agricultural politics, asking himself the question, "Why do farmers live in poverty?" Yanagita loved the tofu of Okinawa, and consumed it as he observed society from the perspective of the common person.

Another person who loved this tofu was Shō Jun. Shō Jun was born in 1875, two years earlier than Yanagita. This Ryukyuan aristocrat, both a cultured man and a business leader, represented the ruling class of Okinawa at the time.

When he was young, Shō Jun wrote an article titled "Tofu no raisan" (In praise of tofu), explaining, "Tofu lovers are derisively referred to as *tōfā*. They are laughed at whenever anyone happens to see them opening their lunchbox only to have raw tofu and tiny salt-pickled fish spill out. It makes the owner of the lunch blush with embarrassment." Shō Jun objected to this behavior and decided to praise tofu to exonerate it from the "false accusations" it suffered.

In this article, Shō Jun praises *tōfuyō*, fermented tofu, as the greatest delicacy in the world:

> If you search throughout this world for foods that can match the good taste of *tōfuyō*, you will find the cheeses of France and the caviar of Russia, as well as *nattō* fermented soybeans and salt-pickled sea urchin (*uni no shiokara*) from Japan. But old cheese is not liked by everyone, while sea urchins and caviar lack the robust, rich flavor of *tōfuyō* and are thus less satisfying. Therefore, I think that *tōfuyō* is one of the best rare delicacies (*chinmi*) in this world—if not the best.[2]

Next, Shō mentions *itami-rokujū* or *age-rokujū*, a dish made of grilled or deep-fried fermented tofu. According to Kaneshiro Sumiko, professor emeritus at the University of the Ryukyus, *itami-rokujū* is named after the *rokujō-dōfu* of Kyoto. It is an Okinawan way of preserving and eating tofu before it goes bad. Right before it spoils, tofu is grilled or fried to make *age-rokujū*. Shō Jun mentions *champuru* (Okinawan stir-fry) made with *itami-rokujū* as a particular delicacy.

Nowadays, *tōfuyō* is well known as an Okinawan specialty and is sold as a souvenir. In the early twentieth century, however, *tōfuyō* was enjoyed only by members of the privileged classes. *Age-rokujū* was mainly eaten by commoners, but became a delicacy for the upper classes.

At the end of his trip across Okinawa, Yanagita went back to Naha and gave a talk titled "Suffering in the World, Suffering on the Isolated Island" at an elementary school in the city. He was invited to the home of Shō Jun in Shuri just a day before his ship departed from Naha. I wonder what the two talked

2. Translation by William Shurtleff and Akiko Aoyagi, from their unpublished *History of Soybeans and Soy Foods*, http://www.soyinfocenter.com/HSS/fermented_tofu1.php.

about on this occasion. The folklorist must have told the aristocrat about his recent observations of tofu on the Nago road.

In the age of Yanagita and Shō Jun, Okinawa was one of the Japanese prefectures sending the largest numbers of immigrants abroad. A great number of commoners immigrated to Hawaii and countries in Central and South America. Although none of the immigrants had much to take with them, some took their hand-operated stone mills for grinding soybeans. With firm resolve, they carried these heavy mills to their new homes, believing their families would survive as long as they could make tofu. Tofu was and still is the staple food for people in Okinawa.

We do not know when tofu was brought to the Ryukyus from its birthplace in China. As Yanagita briefly noted, "In shops like these, bean curds are squeezed and boiled"; thus, Okinawan island tofu was made differently from tofu in Yamato. This may have been because Ryukyuans learned tofu-making directly from the Chinese people, whereas tofu came to Yamato via Korea. This speculation is based on the fact that the Ryukyu Kingdom flourished through trade with China and even had a Ryukyu House, a regional office, in China's Fujian Province.

Handed down directly from China, island tofu "as strong and sturdy as a wandering samurai" met with a crisis in 1972, when Okinawa reverted to Japan. It turned out that the manufacturing method was now in violation of Japan's Food Sanitation Law. Island tofu is made by boiling soymilk with *nigari* and pouring the curds into a mold, then pressing them with a weight. It is then served hot. The hotter the tofu, the fresher it is. On the mainland, tofu is made by immersion in cold water. Okinawans were initially forced to follow the "mainland way" of tofu-making, but they persisted in their protests, and today, Okinawans are allowed to make tofu in the traditional way.

Traditional Okinawan tofu has less moisture than the mainland Japanese type. A block is about three times as large as the standard block of tofu on the mainland.

Dried tofu · *Rokujū*

Rokujū is cured tofu. It has the same properties as tofu.

Rokujū (which means "sixty" in Japanese) is made by cutting tofu into thin slices, sprinkling them with salt, and sun-drying them. These salty, hard slices are difficult to digest. One may eat *rokujū* either grilled or fried in oil. Avoid eating it cold. *Rokujū* should not be eaten by people suffering from any kind of illness.

Age-rokujū *(fried* rokujū*)*

Yaki-rokujū *(grilled* rokujū*)*

Baron Shō Jun, who was an epicurean, wrote in his posthumously published article "In Praise of Tofu" that the very best delicacy made with tofu was *tōfuyō*. *Itami-rokujū* (grilled salt-cured tofu) was second, he wrote. "It's no exaggeration to say *itami-rokujū* is a superlative delicacy when nicely ripened." He also praised *age-rokujū*, made by frying *rokujū* in lard, as a dish that goes well with sake.

What does *itami-rokujū* taste like when "nicely ripened"? As the transcript of *Gozen honzō* says, *rokujū* was made by cutting tofu into thin slices, sprinkling them with salt, and leaving them to dry in the sun almost to the point of spoiling. The slices were then grilled or fried in lard. Shō Jun enjoyed *itami-rokujū* as a delicacy, but commoners had a different perspective. Tofu that was left over or that had gone unsold would already have begun to go bad in the warm weather of Okinawa, so locals washed it in salt water, and the next morning put it in with sweet potatoes they were steaming for breakfast. The steamed tofu was then grilled or fried. For ordinary people, *rokujū* was simply a way of preserving tofu.

Thin Japanese noodles · *Saumen*

Saumen are *sōmen* (thin Japanese noodles). They are sweet, neutral, and nontoxic.

Saumen noodles harmonize the spleen and stomach and enhance qi energy. Eating too many cold noodles produces damp heat, and causes various diseases. Fried noodles cause a fever and thirst. Eating *saumen* in excess is bad for the internal organs.

Incompatible food: Loquat

Rūizōmin

★ Ingredients

Sōmen thin wheat noodles, chicken or pork, eggs beaten and cooked in thin, crepe-like layers, seasoned shiitake mushrooms, string beans or other green vegetables, dashi stock

★ Directions

Boil *sōmen* noodles quickly. Drain the noodles and fold in a bowl. Cut the crepe-like eggs into narrow strips; do the same with the seasoned shiitake and green vegetables. Arrange these ingredients on top of the noodles to create a pleasing balance of colors. Pour cold dashi stock over all to fill the bowl.

Saumen noodles are said to have been introduced to the Ryukyus in the Nara period (710–794). They were described in writing on strips of wood that were excavated from ruins. The original form of *saumen* was made by kneading sticky rice and flour into two thin ropes, twisting them together, and frying them in oil.

Rūizōmin was originally a soup for happy occasions. In my restaurant, I served it as the last dish of the summer course meal. To make *rūizōmin*, fold cooked *saumen* in several layers, add a variety of toppings, and pour cold broth over it. Because of these different ingredients, I initially thought the Chinese character used for *rūi* would be the one meaning "various." In an ancient book, however, it was written using the character for "as you like it." I was embarrassed by my careless assumption.

Wheat gluten •*Fu*

Fu is wheat gluten. It is sweet, cools the body, and is nontoxic.

Fu harmonizes the internal organs, dissipates heat, harmonizes the spleen and stomach, and enhances qi energy. It can be used to treat various illnesses. Persons with fever from chronic fatigue may eat *fu* any time. Frying is said to exacerbate abdominal spasms, so care should be taken.

Kuruma *(wheel-shaped)* fu

Fu champurū (stir-fry with wheat gluten)

★ **Ingredients**

Kuruma fu, eggs, vegetables in season

★ **Directions**

Tear the *kuruma fu* into pieces and soak in water until soft. Gently squeeze out the water, then dip the pieces in beaten egg and fry them with vegetables. Season with salt, pepper, and soy sauce.

Seasoned and fried *fu* tastes like chicken, so it is recommended as a dish for dieters.

The reprint of *Gozen honzō* adds the following description of *fu*: *It is made by kneading bran, flour, and water.* There are two types of *fu*, raw and toasted. Bran, which is the hull of the wheat berry, is separated from the rest of the grain when making flour. In the past, bran was only eaten during famines, and rarely served otherwise. In the past fifty years, however, its value as a dietary fiber is drawing attention, and there has been a revival of interest in bran as a health food.

Rice cake • *Mochi*

Mochi is a soft cake made of pounded sweet (glutinous) rice. It is sweet, warms the body, and is nontoxic.

Mochi warms the internal organs, reduces urine, and causes constipation. Eaten in excess, it damages the spleen and stomach, causes depression, and generates heat. Sick people and children should avoid eating mochi. The Chinese character for mochi refers to the rice after it has been pounded into cakes, as well as when it is stuffed with bean jam.

Nantū is a kind of rice cake that is indispensable at the lunar New Year; children used to receive a piece of *nantū* at New Year's along with a gift of money. It is also said to have been served to customers visiting the red-light district in Naha. *Mūchī* is a fragrant rice cake wrapped in a shell ginger leaf and steamed. It is made on December 8 of the lunar calendar to protect children from evil spirits. *Mūchī* is also called *kāsa mūchī*.

Mūchī (Top in the photo)

★ **Ingredients**
Mochiko sweet rice flour, raw or granulated sugar, shell ginger leaves
★ **Directions**
Dissolve the sugar in hot water. Mix in the rice flour to make a dough. Knead until soft (to about the texture of an earlobe) and then let sit. Divide into pieces and shape into rectangles. Then wrap each in a shell ginger leaf. Tie with a piece of string and steam.

Nantū (Bottom in the photo)

★ **Ingredients**
Mochiko sweet rice flour, brown sugar, *hihatsu* (*Piper longum*, or island pepper) or ginger, miso, shell ginger leaves, shelled peanuts
★ **Directions**
Dissolve the brown sugar in water. Mix in the rice flour to make dough, adding miso and *hihatsu* or ginger for fragrance. Knead until soft (to about the texture of an earlobe). Flatten pieces of the dough into squares and place on individual shell ginger leaves. Steam. Top with peanut halves.

Wheat flour
• *Muginoko*

Muginoko is wheat flour. It is sweet, warms the body, and is slightly toxic.
Flour supplements deficiencies and enhances vitality. Eating it in excess clogs up the stomach and causes constipation, resulting in chronic disease. Use it to make thin *hauhau* (crepes) and wrap them around leeks, bean sprouts, and stewed pork. This dish is called *usumochi* (thin rice cake).

Aburamochi

Aburamochi is a type of dry confection. It is sweet and salty, warms the body, and is nontoxic.
Aburamochi enhances bowel movements and urination, moistens the stomach, warms the internal digestive organs, and enhances qi energy. Eating too much *aburamochi* is detrimental to the spleen and stomach, and causes illness. Sick people and children should avoid eating it.

The word *hauhau* in the eexcerpt on the preceding page refers to the crepe wrapping of *pōpō*, an Okinawan sweet made during the Hārī (dragon-boat race) Festival held on May 4 of the lunar calendar. *Pōpō* is made by mixing flour in water and cooking the batter to make a thin crepe. These crepes are wrapped around *andansu*, which is made by sautéing finely chopped pork with sugar and miso. Tsūkan writes about wrapping stewed pork in crepes, which reminds us of Chinese steamed dumplings. He recommends rolling flour crepes into *hauhau* crepes or wrapping ingredients inside them. At the same time, he warns that eating excessive quantities causes constipation. *Pōpō* is not only eaten at festivals but is also a popular snack food. Okinawans often eat it when taking a break from field work.

Chinbin (recipe below) is an Okinawan-style crepe containing unrefined sugar. *Hanbin* is another variety of *aburamochi*. It is made by mixing sweet rice flour with water, adding baking soda and salt, and then frying the batter in oil. For wedding celebrations, people used to cook large pieces of *hanbin*, put them in a nest of boxes, and take them to the home of newlyweds. *Hanbin* made with unrefined sugar is called *satahanbin*.

Chinbin *(On opposite page)*

★ **Ingredients**
Wheat flour, *mochiko* sweet rice flour, unrefined sugar

★ **Directions**
Dissolve the unrefined sugar in a small amount of water to make a syrup. Mix equal quantities of wheat flour and rice flour in water, then add the syrup to make a runny batter. Grease the pan, place over medium heat, and pour in a thin layer of batter. Keep an eye on the heat as it cooks. When small air bubbles start to appear, flip the crepe over and fry the other side. Remove from heat. Roll the crepe away from you.

Pōpō *(Above)*

★ **Ingredients**
Wheat flour, baking powder, water, *andansu* (a mixture of pork, sugar, and miso)

★ **Directions**
Mix the flour and baking powder with water to make a runny batter. Grease the pan and cook in a thin layer. Spread *andansu* on the crepe, and roll it up away from you.

Gourds and other vegetables
typical of Okinawa. Shown here
are yellow island carrots, a red
sweet potato cut open to show the
purple insides, island chilis smaller
than those on mainland Japan,
purple-leafed Okinawan spinach,
and other vegetables.

Mustard greens · Nā

Nā are mustard greens (*Brassica juncea*). Mustard stems and leaves are pungent and have a warming effect on the body. They are nontoxic.

Mustard greens drive out pathogenic qi from the kidneys, unclog the nine holes, clear the ears and eyes, relax the internal organs, halt coughing and flushing, get rid of chills, clear the lungs, remove phlegm, strengthen the chest, and open the stomach for digestion. Mustard greens with large leaves are good. Narrow, furry leaves are slightly toxic. Mustard greens should be avoided by people with sores or hemorrhoids. Stems and leaves may be pickled in sake lees.

Incompatible food: Rabbit meat, crucian carp

Nā, the Okinawan name for mustard greens, is a popular vegetable also called "island greens." Leaves are fried, pickled (to make *chikina*), or boiled to be served with a soy-sauce dressing.

The "nine holes" in the excerpt refers to the body's orifices: the eyes, ears, nostrils, mouth, and the two for reproduction and excretion. I had never heard of this phrase before and wondered if it was used in traditional Chinese medicine. The excerpt says mustard greens should be avoided by people with sores or hemorrhoids. But this green vegetable enhances qi flow and gets rid of chills, which means it is indispensable for women.

Island greens rice

★ Ingredients
Mustard greens, *aburaage* deep-fried tofu skins, dashi stock, soy sauce, mirin, cooked rice, toasted white sesame seeds
★ Directions
Parboil the mustard greens, drain well, and cut into pieces. Do the same with the deep-fried tofu skins. Lightly oil a pan and stir-fry the mustard greens and tofu. Season with a small amount of dashi stock, soy sauce, and mirin. When the greens are tender, remove from the heat, add to the cooked rice, and mix to combine. To serve, arrange in a bowl and sprinkle white sesame seeds on top.

Fennel · *Mannen-uikyō*

Mannen-uikyō is *Foeniculum vulgare*, or fennel. It is pungent, neutral, and nontoxic.

Fennel treats nausea, stops rumbling in the stomach, and cures muscle cramps in the back and abdomen. It can be used to treat swelling caused by kidney qi failure, which causes piercing pains in the side of the body.

Tsūkan writes that fennel has a good effect on digestive disorders and stomachaches. Fennel is also called *īchōba* in Okinawa and is used to cover up fishy odors.

We do not know when fennel, which is native to Mediterranean coastal areas, was brought to Okinawa. In the West, this herb is often added to fish dishes and salad. Both fennel leaves and flowers have various effects on the body. When this herb grows tall, it bears yellow flowers that look like tiny seeds. Okinawans believe that eating fennel fruits (also called seeds) will keep mosquitoes away. In Europe, chewing fennel fruits is said to be good for losing weight because it freshens the mouth and suppresses hunger.

Īchōba tempura

★ **Ingredients**

Īchōba (fennel) fronds; flour, eggs, and water (for tempura batter); extra flour for dipping; oil for deep-frying

★ **Directions**

Wash fennel and drain. Mix flour, egg, and water to make a loose batter. Dip fennel in flour, and then in batter. Deep-fry in hot oil. Hold the stem with chopsticks and shake gently so that the fine leaves spread out as the fennel is frying. This will keep the batter from becoming lumpy.

Orange daylily · *Kansō*

Kansō is orange daylily (*Hemerocallis fulva*). Both leaves and flowers are sweet. They have a cooling effect on the body and are nontoxic.

Orange daylilies open the chest and relax the five internal organs. The daylily is called a "forget-worry plant" because it prevents sickness even when one eats and drinks excessively. It cures bloody urine and impaired urination, eases a feverish body, treats alcohol-induced jaundice, promotes digestion, improves water metabolism, and cures insomnia. Long-term consumption lightens the body and clears the vision.

Kansō or *kanzō*, a species of daylily, is called *yabukanzō* in Japanese. It grows in fields and bears orange flowers from spring to summer. It is often mistaken for *Lilium maculatum*, another plant in the lily family. The name *daylily* refers to the one-day life of the flower. In China, the plant is called *jīnzhēnhua*, which also means "forget-worry plant."

The young buds and stems are edible; they are usually boiled and served with a soy sauce dressing. The flowers are also edible, and the tubers are used as an herbal medicine. At the restaurant I used to run, we parboiled the petals and then pickled them in sweetened vinegar, or added them to soup to give it a bright color.

Orange daylily with vinegared miso dressing

★ Ingredients
Orange daylily buds (with stems), white miso, sugar, vinegar, mustard

★ Directions
Parboil the orange daylily, then drain and cut into bite-sized lengths. Mix the white miso, sugar, vinegar, and mustard in a mortar until thickened. Arrange the daylilies on a plate and pour the dressing over.

Nigana

Nigana is *Crepidiastrum lanceolatum*, an edible flowering plant in the daisy family. It is bitter, makes the body cold, and is nontoxic.

Nigana, *or* njana *in Okinawa*

Nigana drives out pathogenic qi from the five internal organs and treats digestive problems caused by jaundice. Taken over a long period, this vegetable calms the mind, enhances qi energy, improves intelligence, lightens the body, and prevents aging. It helps resist hunger and cold, harmonizes meridian flow, and increases power. It cures nausea caused by sunstroke. Despite its cooling effect, daily consumption of *nigana* benefits health. Persons with weak digestive functions should not eat too much.

Incompatible food: Honey

In Okinawa, *nigana* is called *njana*, which means "bitter vegetable." A perennial plant that grows on beach rocks, it is called *hosoba-wadan* on mainland Japan (*wadan* is a corruption of *wata no na* which means "plant of the sea" in Japanese). *Njana* is a typical medicinal herb of Okinawa. Its bitter taste conveys untamed nature in a way that vegetables on the mainland no longer do. *Njana* leaves and stems are boiled to make a decoction for stomachaches and diarrhea, a cure still widely employed in Okinawa today. *Njana* is also indispensable in everyday dishes such as squid-ink soup and *shira'ae* (vegetables seasoned with a sweet sauce of tofu and sesame seeds).

Njana shira'ae (On opposite page)

★ Ingredients
Njana, white sesame seeds, tofu, sugar, soy sauce, salt

★ Directions
Grind the sesame seeds in a mortar and mix in the drained tofu. Add sugar, a little soy sauce, and salt to make a slightly sweet dressing. Blanch the *njana* and cut into small pieces, then mix with the dressing.

At my restaurant, we added one more step to bring out the flavor of the greens. After lightly mixing the tofu, sesame seeds, and seasonings in a mortar, we dry-roasted the ingredients in a pan and stirred them with a wooden spoon until the moisture evaporated. This gives the dressing a pulpy texture, which mixes well with finely cut vegetables.

Squid-ink soup (Above)

★ Ingredients
Squid, squid ink, *njana*, dashi stock, salt

★ Directions
Remove the ink sac from the squid. Clean and trim the squid, then cut into round or rectangular slices, or any shape you like. Place the *njana* in the bottom of a saucepan to eliminate the fishy smell of the ink. Pour in the dashi stock, add the ink and squid slices, and simmer until tender. Season with a pinch of salt. The cooking procedure varies among the islands; sometimes the *njana* is added while the other ingredients are simmering.

Japanese mugwort • *Futsuba*

Futsuba is Japanese mugwort (*Artemisia princeps*). It is bitter, warms the body slightly, and is nontoxic.

Mugwort stops vomiting of blood, cures dysentery and bloody uterus flux in women, gets rid of lassitude caused by dampness, strengthens surface muscles, prevents wind-cold, warms the internal organs, cures chills, and eliminates moisture stagnation. This medicinal herb helps women get pregnant. It drives out pathogenic qi from the body and cures genital sores.

Futsuba, pronounced *fūchiba* in Okinawa, refers to Japanese mugwort that grows naturally in fields and mountains. Mugwort leaves are served as tempura or added to rice porridge cooked in pork broth to make a dish called *jūshī*.

Elders in Okinawa are well aware of the herb's medicinal effect. Brewing dried young leaves collected in spring makes a decoction that is good for digestion, as well as the anemia and poor circulation that women often suffer from. Mugwort is also known as the raw material of moxa. I learned that soaking in a bath with a bundle of dried mugwort is good for backaches.

Unfortunately, people on the mainland no longer cook the herb as a side dish; they only mix it in mochi cakes. Mugwort reminds us that vegetables are actually "edible greens growing in the wild."

Fūchiba jūshī rice porridge

★ Ingredients

Rice (dry or cooked), pork broth, salt, soy sauce, *fūchiba* (mugwort)

★ Directions

Fūchiba jūshī is recommended for hangovers. You can use leftover rice, although cooking the porridge from dry rice grains makes it stickier and tastier. Put the rice in a saucepan and pour in the pork broth (if not available, use dashi stock) to cover the rice. Bring to a boil and simmer until the rice thickens. Season with salt and a little soy sauce. Cut up the mugwort and add it to the porridge. The refreshing aroma will settle the stomach.

Okinawan spinach •*Handama*

Handama is Okinawan spinach (*Gynura bicolor*). It is sweet and has a cooling effect on the body. It is nontoxic.

Okinawan spinach cools and activates the blood. People suffering from blood diseases can eat it regularly.

Boiled *handama* (Okinawan spinach) with soy-sauce dressing

Okinawan spinach, which is native to Indonesia, has leaves with a green surface and a reddish-purple backside. When parboiled, this medicinal herb feels both slimy and crunchy in the mouth. In Okinawa, it is known as a blood medicine. It is stir-fried (*irichī*), fried with miso (*nbushī*), or boiled and served with soy-sauce dressing. Okinawan spinach is called *suizenji-na* on mainland Japan (*kintoki-sō* in Kanazawa city). *Honzō kōmoku keimō*, a book on the classification of medicinal herbs published in the late Edo period, describes the origin of the name *suizenji-na*: "Collect the plant's leaves and blanch them in hot water. The blanched leaves will have a texture as flexible as *suizenji-nori* (an edible species of freshwater blue-green algae). This is why the herb is named *suizenji-na*."

★ **Ingredients**
Handama spinach, dashi stock, soy sauce

★ **Directions**
Blanch the *handama*, noting that it will lose its reddish-purple color after boiling. Avoid overcooking; drain quickly. Mix together the dashi stock and soy sauce to taste and pour over the *handama* to dress (do not add undiluted soy sauce directly to the greens). Enjoy the contrasting textures of the vegetable.

Suizenji-na, *or* handama *in Okinawa*

71

Mung bean sprouts · *Oyashi*

Oyashi are mung bean sprouts. They are sweet, neutral, and nontoxic.

Mung bean sprouts detoxify alcohol-induced heat and harmonize the qi energy of triple energizers. They are grown with damp heat, and therefore have a different nature from mung beans. Eating *oyashi* in excess causes sores.

Oyashi refers to mung bean sprouts, which are called *māmina* in Okinawa. These sprouts are used in *champurū* Okinawan stir-fry, as well as in Japanese-style mixed salad tossed with dressing. Mung beans sprout when placed in a basket and soaked in water. *Gozen honzō* explains that the *oyashi* "grow in damp heat" and have a different effect on the body from mung beans. The "triple energizers" referred to in the excerpt is a collective term for the "six bowels" cited in Chinese medicine; these have no analog in Western medicine. In Chinese medicine, there are three types of body energizers—referred to as upper, middle, and lower—that control digestion, absorption, and evacuation respectively. Today, some people think the term "triple energizers" refers to hormones and lymphatic vessels. They are also interpreted as the three burners of life. Considering this, it could be said that *māmina* sprouts are a food for activating the inside of the body.

Māmina and *mimigā* dressed with miso and vinegar

★ **Ingredients**
Māmina (bean sprouts), *mimigā* (pig ear), peanut butter, sweet miso, vinegar, sugar

★ **Directions**
Wash and parboil the bean sprouts. Cut the pig ear into small pieces, wash, and parboil. Combine the peanut butter, sweet miso, vinegar, and sugar to make a dressing. Pour over the sprouts and pig ear to serve.

Peucedanum japonicum • Bōfū

Bōfū is *Peucedanum japonicum*. It tastes sweet, warms the body, and is nontoxic.

Bōfū treats colds, stops headaches, and cures conjunctivitis, as well as body aches caused by a cold. Long-term consumption reduces wind-dampness and lightens the body. The stems must not be consumed.

Bōfū grows naturally in Okinawa. The Japanese name is *botan-bōfū*, but the herb differs from *hama-bōfū*, or beach silvertop, often used as a garnish for sashimi. In Okinawa, this herb is called *safuna* or "long-life plant." It has a unique aroma. When used as a traditional medicine for colds, it is brewed with pork kidneys to make a decoction. As it contains much carotene and other vitamins, this medicinal herb is said to have an antioxidizing effect. I'm not sure who nicknamed *safuna* the "long-life plant," but the herb is true to its name.

Botan-bōfū, *also known as* Peucedanum japonicum *and long-life plant*

Safuna shira'ae (safuna dressed with tofu)

★ Ingredients

Safuna; dashi stock; tofu, sugar, soy sauce, mirin, salt (for dressing)

★ Directions

Blend together the drained tofu and seasonings in a mortar and dry roast. Wash the *safuna* thoroughly and cut its leaves. Parboil and immerse in dashi stock. Drain lightly and mix with the tofu dressing. Serve on a plate. Enjoy the aroma and bitter taste of this salad-like dish.

Yellow carrot · *Kidaikon*

Kidaikon is yellow carrot (*Daucus carota*). The root is sweet and pungent, has a slight warming effect on the body, and is nontoxic.

Yellow carrot harmonizes the internal organs, activates qi energy, strengthens the chest, unblocks the bowels, and relaxes the five internal organs. Eating this root vegetable only benefits people; there is nothing to lose from eating it. It should, however, be avoided by people with spleen deficiency or diarrhea.

Kidaikon, or *chidēkuni* in the Okinawan dialect, is a yellow carrot unique to Okinawa Island, and ranks as a delicacy alongside the red Kyoto carrot. It is native to Central Asia; the original Chinese name means something like "root vegetable brought from a foreign country, eaten like a daikon radish." A yellow carrot is not a daikon, but it is a common Okinawan winter root vegetable.

Island carrots

Chidēkuni shiri-shiri

★ **Ingredients**
Chidēkuni (yellow carrot), soy sauce, mirin, dashi stock

★ **Directions**
Cut the yellow carrot into thin matchsticks or shred on a *shiri-shiri*. Oil the pan, stir-fry the carrot slices, and season with mirin and soy sauce. Add a small amount of dashi stock and continue to cook until the carrots are tender.

A *shiri-shiri* is a kind of mandoline or grater used for slicing or shredding vegetables. It can be bought in Okinawa, where it is often used to slice up carrots and papayas. (The term *shiri-shiri* is sometimes used in cooking to mean "scraping.") The mandoline slicers common in mainland Japan and elsewhere have a thin blade, which is useful for making slivered garnishes for sashimi and the like. A long slicer with small cutting holes is also popular. The Okinawan *shiri-shiri* slicer has rather large holes. Gently run a carrot or papaya against the blade to cut the fruit or vegetable to just the right length and thickness. This implement is helpful for people without knife skills.

Island chilis · *Kōraigoshō*

Kōraigoshō, or *Capsicum frutescens*, are chili peppers. They are pungent, warm the body, and are nontoxic.
Chilis enhance the digestion of food and drink accumulated in the stomach, open the stomach, remove pathogenic qi, and freshen fishy breath. Eating too many causes sores and ulcers.

A modern Japanese reading of the reprinted *Gozen honzō* says: "Chilis are called 'Kōryo (Korean dynasty) peppers,' or more commonly 'Chinese peppers' or 'European peppers.'" The word *kōraigoshō* means "peppers from a barbarian (or foreign) country." Okinawan chilis are small and very pungent. They belong to a different species from their Japanese counterparts. As the name denotes, Okinawan chilis are thought to have come from China or Korea. They are used in a variety of dishes that warm the body when the weather is cold, and cool it down in the heat. Okinawans preserve island chilis in *awamori* rice liquor to make *kōrēgusu*. This spicy seasoning is said to have been inspired by the chili-pepper water of Hawaii, where many immigrants from Okinawa lived before World War II. Today, *kōrēgusu* is used as a condiment for Okinawan soba.

Fried and marinated *gurukun* (banana fish) with chili peppers

★ Ingredients
Gurukun banana fish, flour, oil for frying, dashi stock, soy sauce, mirin, vinegar, island chilis, roasted leeks or sliced onions

★ Directions
Fillet the fish. Score each fillet for even heating in oil. Dredge both sides in flour and fry. Make a spicy sauce by mixing the dashi stock, soy sauce, mirin, vinegar, and chopped chilis. Marinate the fish in the sauce overnight. Add roasted leek or onion slices, if available. Serve.

Chinese onion
• *Rakkyō*

Rakkyō is Chinese onion (*Allium chinense*). It is bitter and pungent. It warms and soothes the body, and is nontoxic.

Eating boiled *rakkyō* harmonizes the internal organs, supplements deficiencies, stops prolonged diarrhea, and builds up the body. Recommended as a regular food for people with heart disease. Women benefit from eating *rakkyō* after childbirth. It cures women's uterine bleeding and vaginal discharge. It is also good for treating incisions. Long-term consumption will make the body light and resistant to hunger, aging, deterioration, and wind-cold. It also helps keep small bones from getting caught in the throat. Persons suffering from febrile disease should refrain from eating in excess. Fresh *rakkyō* should not be eaten in March and April.

Incompatible foods: Beef, ginger

Rakkyō, a pungent bulb in the allium family which is native to China, is grown on mainland Japan. When used as food, it is pickled in sweet vinegar or soy sauce and served as a garnish for rice with curry sauce. Island *rakkyō* produced in Okinawa is slightly smaller and thinner than its mainland equivalent, and has a unique pungent taste. This shallot-like bulb can be served lightly salted or fried as tempura.

Rakkyō is used as a natural drug in Chinese herbal medicine. It is said to remove weight and pain from the chest. Tsūkan describes it as a medicine to treat heart disease and incised wounds.

Rakkyō *preserved in miso*

Rakkyō *preserved in salt*

Island *rakkyō* tempura

★ Ingredients
Island *rakkyō*, flour, water, egg, salt, oil for deep-frying
★ Directions
Peel and wash the *rakkyō*. Mix flour with a little water and add egg and a pinch of salt to make a batter. Dip *rakkyō* in the batter and deep-fry until golden.

Unwashed island rakkyō

Sweet potato • *Hantsun-imo*

Hantsun-imo is a sweet potato (*Ipomoea batatas*).

Sweet potatoes are sweet. They make the spleen and stomach healthy, nourish deficiencies, and strengthen the yin aspect of the kidney. Eat them daily to live a long life.

Taro stems and leaves
• *Imonoha*

Imonoha are the stems and leaves of the taro plant.

Taro stems and leaves settle the stomach, unblock the bowels, and promote defecation. Always eat them as vegetables.

The reprinted *Gozen honzō* mentions a different name for the sweet potato, but does not include Tsūkan's phrase "*hantsun-imo* is a sweet potato" as quoted here. The first Chinese character means "gastronomy," and one part of this character implies "tasty." I wonder if this word was coined by privileged classes who lived in Shuri, the capital of the Ryukyu Kingdom. Sweet potatoes were introduced to the Ryukyus in 1605, about two hundred years before *Gozen honzō* was written. These potatoes, called *nmu* by commoners, saved people from starvation during repeated famines. They were also necessary as fodder for pigs.

The stem of the taro plant, called *kandabā* in Okinawa, is cooked to make *jūshī* (rice gruel) and *nbushī* (miso-simmered) dishes. Most Japanese people ate taro stems and leaves in the lean years after World War II. But after the country rose from the ashes of the war, this food was quickly forgotten on the mainland. Only Okinawans continue to eat and enjoy *kandabā*.

Steamed sweet potatoes

Sweet potato: Potatoes with a history

When I hear the word *imo*, or "potato," I first think of the sweet-potato rice my grandmother used to cook for me when we lived on an old back street in Tokyo. The hot, flaky bits of potato mixed in the rice tasted like chestnuts. When I was small, my grandmother often told me scary Buddhist stories. But when sweet-potato rice was on the table, she always told me a story of three men in the Edo period. I thought she made up the story herself, but I later found the original in a school textbook, and it was not much different from her version. In my mind, I can still clearly hear her narrative in the high-flown style of traditional Japanese storytelling.

The story goes like this. Ōoka Echizen, a magistrate of Edo, saw talent in Aoki Konyō, a low-ranking samurai. To put Aoki's abilities to good use, Ōoka referred him to the shogun Tokugawa Yoshimune, who was dealing with a major famine. Aoki recommended sweet potatoes as a hardy crop that would feed the hungry. Tokugawa immediately ordered the Satsuma domain to supply sweet-potato cuttings and put Aoki in charge of learning to cultivate them in the Koishikawa Botanical Gardens. The variety developed by Aoki was later named *satsuma-imo* (*imo* means potato). It spread throughout Japan, saving the population from starvation. What my grandmother never told me was how the sweet potato got to Satsuma in the first place.

It turns out that *satsuma-imo* is a vegetable with a historic background. We can trace it back to when it was taken to China from its origins in Central America, and then to the Ryukyus, where cultivation of sweet potatoes started in 1605. A record[3] says an officer from the Ryukyus returned home from Fujian in China with seedlings. Later, Gima Shinjō, the steward of Gima village, promoted sweet-potato cultivation throughout the Ryukyus.

In 1705, exactly one hundred years later, the Ryukyuan potato found its way to mainland Japan. Satsuma fisherman Maeda Riu'emon learned in Ryukyu how to cultivate sweet potatoes by grafting and brought them home with him. Tokugawa Yoshimune and Aoki Konyō didn't come along until about thirty years later, in 1734. Thus, sweet potatoes were brought from China to the Ryukyu Islands, then from Satsuma to Edo and the entire country.

The name *satsuma-imo* became popular nationwide in the early twentieth century. Before then, the sweet potato had been called by many names in

---

3. *Ryukyu-koku yurai-ki* [The official chorography of the Ryukyu Kingdom], section on sweet potatoes, *Ryukyu-koku kyū-ki*, *Kyūyō*, etc.

different regions. For example, the Okinawan name was *nmu* or *akkon*. In *The History of Sweet Potatoes*,[4] author Miyamoto Tsuneichi writes: "The term '*Ryukyu-imo*' was used rather widely [note: in the Kanto area of the mainland]. It was also used by Richard Cox.[5] The name obviously denotes the original home of the vegetable, and many people used it for potatoes supplied directly from the Ryukyus or grown around Hirado, a city located in northern Kyushu." This book also gives many other names: *kōkō-imo* on Tsushima Island, *kara-imo* (Chinese potato) in Shikoku, *rikiu-imo* (*rikiu* is a corruption of the word Ryukyu) in Kyoto, and *hama-imo* along the coast of the Sea of Japan.

The book *Kainan Shōki* by Yanagita Kunio, mentioned earlier in the section on tofu, starts with an essay titled "Sweet-Potato Regions." It briefly explains the history of these names:

A reader for fifth graders in primary school says, "The name of sweet potatoes varies by region. They are called *satsuma-imo* in the Kanto region, *Ryukyu-imo* in Satsuma, and *kara-imo* in the Ryukyus. These different names tell us that the potato came from the West." This description, however, is not exactly correct. Ryukyuans commonly call sweet potatoes *nmu*, not *kara-imo*. *Nmu* means "our potato." *Kara-imo* or *tau-imo* is commonly used in southern Kyushu.

Woman carrying her purchase of sweet potatoes, Ryukyu fūzoku ezu *(Ryukyuan manners and customs illustrated), edition published in 1982 in Japanese (Hawley Collection Compilation Committee, vol. 5), courtesy of Sakamaki and Hawley Collection, University of Hawaii at Manoa*

No one in Satsuma says *Ryukyu-imo*, which is the name widely used in part of northern Kyushu, western Honshu, and the Kyoto-Osaka district. Nowadays, these names are disappearing with the universal adoption of *satsuma-imo*.[6]

---

4. "The History of Sweet Potatoes," in *Nihon minshū-shi* [Japanese popular history] vol. 7, by Miyamoto Tsuneichi (Miraisha, 1962).

5. Chief of the British trading post in Hirado, Nagasaki Prefecture. Richard Cox is said to have started farming sweet potatoes in Hirado in 1615.

6. "Meals in Okinawa based upon oral recollections," in *Nihon no shokuseikatsu zenshū 47* [Collection of 47 articles on the Japanese diet] (Rural Culture Association Japan, 1977]

The reader quoted by Yanagita is from the turn of the twentieth century. I wonder how many people were saved from starvation by sweet potatoes when famines struck the country. Even prior to the lean years at the end of World War II, commoners in Okinawa had long lived on potatoes. A book on Japanese diet vividly describes the way women in Itoman city cooked sweet potatoes for their households.

Even during the coldest days of winter, housewives wake up around four o'clock in the morning to boil *umu* [an alternate pronunciation of *nmu*] in a big iron pot. In Itoman, there are no irrigated rice fields, so locals grow *umu*, which they eat as their staple food throughout the year. Housewives wash the potatoes before going to bed. The next morning, while it is still dark, they go to the garden well to fetch water to fill the pot. They boil a lot of potatoes because they need enough to feed their families and livestock for the entire day. To fire up the *umu* hearth and get the water boiling, women spread rice hulls on the hearth bed, put small bundles of dried plants on them, and burn them while stirring the whole with a *hītangusā* bamboo stick.

After the war, Okinawans, like most Japanese, switched to a rice-based diet. Yet, even today, *umu* is served often, and its leaves are prepared as a side dish. Actually, the leaves are indispensable for making the rice gruel called *kandabā-jūshī* and as an ingredient in miso soup.

Sweet potato vendor, Ryukyu fūzoku ezu
(Ryukyuan manners and customs illustrated)

Taro · *Ta-imo*

Ta-imo, or *Colocasia esculenta,* is a type of taro grown in paddy fields. It tastes like taro root (pungent, neutral, and slightly toxic).

Taro grown in water causes disorders that produce damp heat. It should be strictly avoided by patients suffering from various diseases. Consumption is allowed in winter, from January to February, but not in the other months.

Ta-imo, also called *tānmu*, is a taro cultivated in paddy fields; the parent taro is eaten. A taro plant produces many offshoot tubers, so it is a symbol of fertility, and is indispensable for celebratory dishes. Because parent tubers grow in small numbers, they are expensive in Okinawa. Fried and cooked *tānmu* is something that is almost always seen on the *tundābun* tray at weddings and other important occasions (see pages 4–5).

Steamed tānmu

Duruwakashī

★ **Ingredients**

Tānmu (taro), taro stem (if available), boiled pork, dried shiitake mushrooms, *kamaboko* steamed fish paste, island carrot, green peas, salt, pork broth

★ **Directions**

Reconstitute the dried shiitake by soaking in cool water for an hour. Taro roots sold in the market have already been steamed. Peel each one carefully by hand and cut into small cubes. Peel and parboil the taro stem, and then cut into pieces. Dice the boiled pork, reconstituted dried mushrooms, carrots, and *kamaboko*. Oil the pan with lard, stir-fry the cut ingredients and green peas, then add the pork broth, and finally the taro cubes. When they are tender, stir with a wooden spoon and season with a pinch of salt. This dish should be seasoned simply so as not to spoil the rich taste of the taro.

Tānmu dengaku (sweet taro)

★ **Ingredients**

Tānmu, Okinawan black sugar, mirin, salt

★ **Directions**

Peel a taro root carefully by hand and cut into large cubes. Simmer the taro cubes and black sugar in just enough water to cover. Cook until the water is gone, and then mix with a wooden spoon until the taro is glazed with sugar. Season with black sugar, mirin, and a pinch of salt.

Wax gourd · *Tōgai*

Tōgai is wax gourd (*Benincasa hispida*). It is sweet, makes the body cold, and is nontoxic.
Wax gourd reduces heat, strengthens the spleen, promotes urination, unblocks the bowels, reduces edema, assuages thirst, and dissipates swelling caused by heat toxins. However, people who are thin should not eat it in excess. Green-skinned wax gourds should not be eaten in September and the preceding months.

Incompatible food: Fried mochi

The wax gourd is native to Southeast Asia and India. In Japan, the characters of its name mean "winter gourd" because the vegetable can be stored and eaten from summer to winter as long as it is kept in a cool place. In Okinawa, the wax gourd has been called *shibui* for some time. For its cooling and diuretic effects, it is often used in herbal medicine foods. Okinawans use wax gourds frequently, even putting them in miso soup. They are valuable in summer when greens cannot sprout due to the heat.

Tōgai *wax gourd*

Shibui in pork soup

★ Ingredients

Pork (bone-in meat may be used), *shibui* wax gourd, pork broth, dashi stock, salt, soy sauce, *awamori* rice liquor, mirin

★ Directions

Cut the pork into bite-size pieces and parboil (skim off the scum and reserve the broth). Peel the wax gourd and cut the flesh into fairly large cubes. Mix the pork broth with dashi stock and add the pork meat and wax gourd. Cook until tender, skimming off the scum that rises to the surface. Season with salt, soy sauce, *awamori*, and mirin.

Bitter melon · *Gōya*

Gōya is bitter melon (*Momordica charantia*). It is bitter and sweet, neutral, and nontoxic.

Bitter melon removes pathogenic heat, reduces fatigue, cleanses the mind, and clears the vision. Bitter melon can be eaten every day during the summer months.

Incompatible food: Fried mochi

On the mainland, people used to call bitter melon *tsurureishi*, but it is now known throughout Japan as *gōya*, the name used in an Okinawan dialect. Momordicin, the bitter component contained in *gōya*, has a stomachic effect and is said to reduce summer fatigue. Today, *gōya* is grown not only in Okinawa but all over the country. The Okinawan *gōya* cultivated in red soil under the hot sun has attractive bright-green skin covered in small bumps. This summer vegetable grown in its birthplace is the pride of Okinawa.

Gōya *bitter melon*

Gōya dressed with dried mullet roe

★ **Ingredients**

Gōya bitter melon, salt, dashi stock, dried mullet roe (bottarga)

★ **Directions**

Cut the *gōya* lengthwise and spoon out the seeds and pith. Slice into thin crescents and sprinkle with salt. Parboil, then drain well. Cover with dashi stock and garnish with dried mullet roe. Serve.

Blanched *gōya* with soy-sauce dressing

★ **Ingredients**

Gōya bitter melon, salt, dashi stock, soy sauce, *katsuobushi* shaved dried bonito or tuna fish

★ **Directions**

Follow the steps above for slicing, parboiling, and draining *gōya*. Combine the dashi stock and soy sauce and pour over the *gōya*. Sprinkle with shavings of dried bonito or tuna.

Grilled *gōya*

★ **Ingredients**

Gōya, oil for deep-frying, *andansu* (miso mixed with pork fat and sugar; see page 63)

★ **Directions**

Cut the *gōya* lengthwise and spoon out the seeds and pith. Lightly rinse and pat dry. Briefly deep-fry each *gōya* half to lock the flavor inside. Grill the fried *gōya* for a short time over an open flame to burn off the oil. Allow to cool slightly, then cut into bars, crescents, or any shape desired. Serve with *andansu*.

Sponge gourd · *Nābera*

**Nābera is sponge gourd (*Luffa cylindrica*).
It is sweet, neutral, and nontoxic.**

Sponge gourds get rid of heat, support the intestines, warm the stomach, and reinforce yang. They stabilize emotions and calm the uterus. Safe for pregnant women.

Incompatible food: Fried mochi

The sponge gourd (known as a loofah in the West) is called *itouri* (thread gourd) in Japanese because its mature fruit is fibrous. But it is more commonly known as *hechima*, a name coined in the Edo period as a play on words. The Okinawan word *nābera* is said to come from "washing the *nabe* (cooking pan)." Young sponge gourds and bitter melons are typical summer vegetables in Okinawa. When fully ripened, *nābera* is dried and used to make body scrubbers.

> *Nābera nbushī* (sponge gourd cooked in miso)

★ **Ingredients**

Nābera (young sponge gourd), pork, miso, dashi stock, tofu

★ **Directions**

Scrape the skin from the sponge gourd with a knife and cut into round slices of desired thickness. Slice the pork thinly and cover with miso. Oil the pan and stir-fry the gourd slices with the pork. Pour in the dashi stock and add large pieces of tofu. Simmer until the gourd produces a thick juice, which will give the dish a distinctive sweet flavor.

Nābērā dengaku (sponge gourd coated with miso sauce)

Okinawans eat nābērā *sponge gourd when it is young and tender, but it is not used as a vegetable in mainland Japan. Once you eat it, though, you will never forget its delicate sweetness, earthy aroma, and soft texture. The recipe given here is tasty and easy to make.*

★ Ingredients
Nābērā (young sponge gourd), oil for deep-frying, miso, ground sesame seeds, sugar, poppy seeds (optional)

1

Wash the *nābērā* and pat dry. On a cutting board, scrape off the skin with a knife, being careful to leave some of the greenish color on the flesh.

2

Cut into pieces 3 to 4 cm thick.

3

Score the top surface of each slice with a cross.

4

Deep-fry the *nābera* slices for about one minute, or until the inside is cooked.

5

Drain on paper towels.

6

Mix the miso with the ground sesame seeds and sugar to make a paste. Use a spatula to coat each piece of *nābera* with the paste.

7

Arrange on a baking tray and bake for one or two minutes in the oven.

8

The photo shows *nābera* coated with miso sauce. Sprinkle with a few poppy seeds if you like.

Bottle gourd (calabash gourd)
• *Tsuburu*

Tsuburu is bottle gourd (*Lagenaria siceraria*). It is sweet, neutral, and nontoxic.

Bottle gourd cures gonorrhea in women, treats bad sores and painful inflammation in the nose and mouth, and promotes urination. It relieves symptoms of beriberi, poor circulation, and chills. Eating bottle gourd in excess causes vomiting and diarrhea.

Incompatible food: Fried mochi

Okinawan yellow cucumber
• *Mofu'uri*

Mofu'uri is Okinawan yellow cucumber (*Cucumis sativus*). It is sweet, makes the body cold, and is nontoxic.

Okinawan yellow cucumber strengthens the stomach and intestines, relieves thirst, promotes urination, and removes alcohol toxins. Eating raw yellow cucumber cools the internal organs, activates qi, and causes heart palpitations. It should not be consumed after outbreaks of infectious disease.

Incompatible food: Fried mochi

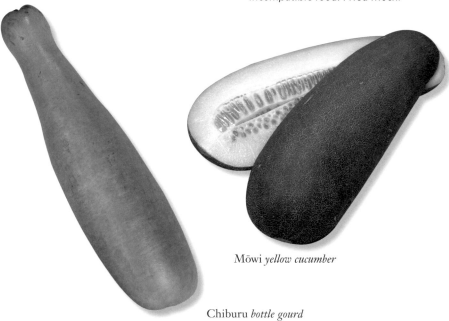

Mōwi *yellow cucumber*

Chiburu *bottle gourd*

The reprint of *Gozen honzō* adds a description of the bottle gourd as "an annual plant that belongs to the species *Lagenaria siceraria*. It is called *tsuboro* in Okinawa and by many other names in other places." These days, Okinawans call the gourd *chiburu*. I wonder when and how the name evolved from *tsuburu* to *tsuboro* to *chiburu*?

Bottle gourds come in larger-fruiting and smaller-fruiting varieties. The latter is mainly used to make dried *kanpyō* strips. Okinawans eat young bottle gourds of the larger variety.

Mofu'uri is called *mōuri* or *mōwi* in Okinawa. The flesh of this Okinawan yellow cucumber has a faintly sweet aroma.

Simmered *chiburu* and *mōwi*

★ **Ingredients**
Chiburu (bottle gourd), *mōwi* (Okinawan yellow cucumber), soy sauce, sugar, mirin, salt, dashi stock

★ **Directions**
Wash a bottle gourd and a yellow cucumber. Cut them lengthwise and spoon out the pith. Cut into slices of equal width. Season the vegetables lightly so as not to overwhelm their subtle smell and flavor. Add the slices to a pot of dashi stock and cook slowly over medium heat.

Kombu · *Konbu*

Kombu is a type of kelp (*Laminariaceae*). It is salty, cools and soothes the body, and is nontoxic.

Kombu cures twelve types of edema, dissipates swelling, eases abdominal spasms and swelling, promotes urination, gets rid of facial swelling, and treats various types of eczema and rashes. It contains a large quantity of iodine and is used to produce that chemical element. Kombu stock, with its pleasant aroma, is widely used in foods for people who are ill.

Kūbu irichī (braised kombu)

★ Ingredients
Kombu, pork, *konnyaku*, *kamaboko* steamed fish paste, sugar, soy sauce, pork broth
★ Directions
Soak dried kombu in water until soft. Wipe dry, then cut into thin slices. Parboil the pork, *konnyaku*, and *kamaboko*, and then slice them to desired thickness. Stir-fry in an oiled pan, adding sugar and soy sauce to taste. Remove ingredients and add the sliced kombu to the same pan with the residue of the seasoning. Pour in the pork broth and boil until kombu is soft. Return the other ingredients to the pan. Simmer until only a little liquid remains.

Kombu: An exceptional trade item

Okinawa was long the top prefecture for consumption of kombu in Japan, although it produced none at all. Recently, it has slipped into twelfth place, and Toyama Prefecture is now number one.[7] Despite this state of affairs, kombu remains as popular an ingredient as pork in Okinawan cuisine.

When and how did Okinawa—at the southernmost end of Japan—begin to buy kombu from Hokkaido, the northernmost island? Why is so much of it consumed today? Tracing the history of kombu, we can see how the Ryukyu Kingdom thrived through transit trade with many Asian countries. A description of the kingdom at its height is inscribed on the Bridge of Nations Bell, which once hung in the main hall of Shuri Castle:

> The Ryukyu Kingdom is a splendid place in the South Sea. It collects superb goods from Korea. Its close relations with China are like those between the upper and lower jaws. Those with Japan are like those between the lips and the teeth.

Kombu from Hokkaido emerged at the center stage of Ryukyu's trade with China in the nineteenth century, when cargo ships called *kitamaebune* (northern-bound ships) revolutionized Japan's shipping logistics. To tell the history of kombu, let me start out with the story of a wealthy merchant in Edo.

The merchant's name was Kawamura Zuiken.[8] In 1670, he was ordered by the Tokugawa shogunate to establish a sea route for vessels to carry goods from northeast Japan down the Pacific coast to Edo, which he did. Two years later, he opened up another sea route to transport goods from Sakata, in modern-day Yamagata Prefecture, down the Sea of Japan coast and through the Seto Inland Sea to Osaka. This allowed *kitamaebune* ships to transport large quantities of seafood, including kombu, from Hokkaido to Osaka. A food culture emerged in Osaka that featured Hokkaido produce, such as the use of dried kombu for making stock and dishes like kombu simmered in soy sauce (*tsukudani*) and herring soba. The sea routes developed by Zuiken

---

7. Ranking by prefectural capital (average of the periods from 2005 to 2007), *Family Income and Expenditure Survey* by the Statistics Bureau of Japan, the Ministry of Internal Affairs and Communications.

8. Kawamura Zuiken (1618–99) was born the son of a poor farmer in Ise. He went to Edo at the age of thirteen and worked as a foreman for public works projects. When the great fire of Meireki (1657) occurred, Zuiken bought up Kiso mountain timber to rebuild houses and made an enormous fortune for himself. Later, under orders from the shogunate, he established *kitamaebune* sea routes for cargo vessels, contributing to the development of Japan's maritime transport in the Edo period.

revolutionized distribution in the early Edo period.

Kombu caught the eye of merchants in the Satsuma domain. They exchanged sugar for kombu and exported it via Ryukyu tributary trade to China, where no kombu was produced.[9] In return, Satsuma merchants imported raw silk, textiles, and herbal medicines from China.

Kombu rolls

★ **Ingredients**
Dried kombu, fresh bonito, dried *kanpyō* strips, sugar, soy sauce, *awamori* rice liquor or sake, mirin

★ **Directions**
Soak the dried kombu in water until soft. Remove kombu, reserving soaking water for later use, and wipe dry. Slice to desired width. Soak the dried *kanpyō* strips in water, knead with salt, and rinse. Cut the bonito into chunks, and then parboil. Wrap each chunk of bonito in a piece of kombu and tie the bundle closed with a *kanpyō* strip. Arrange the kombu rolls on a very thin sheet of wood or a large piece of kombu placed on the bottom of a large saucepan. Pour in the reserved kombu soaking water to barely cover the rolls. Bring to a boil, then simmer for about one hour, seasoning with sugar, soy sauce, *awamori* or sake, and mirin. Simmer until kombu is tender and has absorbed the seasonings.

This trade is described in the *Ryukyu Okinawa-shi no sekai* (The historical world of Ryukyu and Okinawa)[10] as follows:

> Chinese medicines imported by Satsuma via the Ryukyus were attractive to medicine peddlers in Toyama. The Satsuma domain supplied Chinese medicines to Toyama merchants in exchange for large amounts of kombu (*Sakoku to han boeki* [Seclusion and trade by domain] by Uehara Kaneyoshi). The kombu was thus brought by Satsuma to the Ryukyus.

According to one record,[11] kombu accounted for 70 to 80 percent of the goods carried by *kitamaebune* vessels in 1820 and afterwards. The total amount was about 10 percent of the kombu produced in Hokkaido. In the nineteenth century, an enormous amount of kombu was collected in Naha, where Satsuma opened up the Kombu Exchange Center and appointed a resident

---

9. In the Chinese tributary system, foreign leaders sent tributes to the Chinese emperor to pledge their allegiance. Ryukyu kings sent envoys bearing gifts and letters. These envoys had an audience with the emperor in Beijing and received a variety of gifts in return. While staying in Beijing, Ryukyuan missions were allowed to trade with Chinese merchants.
10. Japanese history 18 compiled by Tomiyama Kazuyuki, *Ryukyu okinawa-shi no sekai* (The historical world of Ryukyu and Okinawa), vol. 2: The structure and logistics network of Ryukyu Trade (Yoshikawa Koubunkan, 2003).
11. *Shindai chūryū kankei tōan senhen* (Chinese title: *Qingdai zhongliu guanxi dang'an xuanbian*; A historical record of goods loaded on Ryukyuan ships).

magistrate to manage it.

Meanwhile, in Satsuma, chief retainer Zusho Hirosato[12] is said to have allowed Satsuma merchants to smuggle kombu to sell to China. These ill-gotten profits helped him rebuild the domain's finances and fill up the war chest in preparation for the Meiji Restoration. The Ryukyu Kingdom, however, did not stand aside and let the Satsuma clan get away with enormous profits from kombu. It set up the Ryukyu House near Kagoshima Castle as its agency. In 1797, a Satsuma merchant who was a creditor of the Ryukyu House applied for a monopoly of the kombu trade. In opposition, a record keeper in the Ryukyu House wrote "Kombu is an exceptional trade item for the Ryukyus. Monopolization will do harm in the future."[13]

Kombu collected in Naha was sorted by quality. Eventually substandard grades and black-market kombu smuggled in by officials spread to not only the privileged classes but also to ordinary Ryukyuans. In the age before refrigeration, dried kombu was a precious food for people living on the subtropical islands. It was a popular gift for festive occasions, as well as the main ingredient of various dishes such as *kūbu irichī* (braised kombu) and *tibichi* (pig-trotter stew). Kombu goes well with pork, the favorite meat of Okinawans, which also spurred its rise in popularity.

The Kombu Exchange Center operated to the west of Naha, near the head office of the present-day Radio Okinawa, until the Ryukyu government was disbanded at the beginning of the Meiji period. After the Ryukyu Annexation, the center of kombu trade with China was relocated by Chinese officers to Hakodate in Hokkaido. These officers had accompanied Matthew C. Perry, a US Navy commander, on his voyage to Hakodate following his famous mission to force Japan to end its seclusion policy.

Why did China have such a great desire to continue importing kombu? Before relying on Ryukyu's tributary trade, China had procured kombu from Dejima, a Dutch trading post in Nagasaki, but it was of poor quality. Chinese people preferred high-quality kombu that had been sorted and graded in the Ryukyus.

In China, kombu was mainly used to make iodine, a chemical element indispensable for humans—in particular, for the synthesis of thyroid hormones. People on the Chinese continent had few opportunities to get iodine, and a great deal of it was needed to treat diseases caused by iodine deficiencies, such

---

12. Zusho Hirosato (1776–1848): Adopted by Zusho Kiyonobu in 1788 and sent to Edo as a tea assistant in 1798. Shimazu Shigehide, the retired lord of Satsuma, recognized Zusho's abilities and gave him further responsibilities. Zusho later served Shimazu Narioki, and in 1838 was appointed chief retainer of the Satsuma domain, in which position he worked to rebuild the domain's finances.

13. Japanese history 18 compiled by Tomiyama Kazuyuki, *Ryukyu okinawa-shi no sekai* (The historical world of Ryukyu and Okinawa), vol. 2: The structure and logistics network of Ryukyu Trade (Yoshikawa Koubunkan, 2003).

as Basedow's goiter. Now, however, those days are over. Whereas it was once a big importer of kombu, China has recently become a leading cultivator as well as exporter of it. How did this happen? Behind this transformation was a Japanese engineer named Ōtsuki Yoshirō.[14]

In 1932, Japan established Manchukuo, a puppet state, in northeast China and Inner Mongolia. To promote industry there, the Japanese government set up the Kwantung Experimental Fishery Station in Dalian. Ōtsuki Yoshirō was sent there as an engineer. On his way from Japan to China, he saw wakame seaweed growing on raw timber towed by a ship. Inspired by this scene, he started experimenting with the cultivation of wakame and kombu. In September 1943, he obtained Japanese patents for farming wakame and kombu on rafts and preserving them in salt. After World War II, at the request of the Chinese government, Ōtsuki took a position as head of an experimental fishery station in Shandong, a northern coastal province in eastern China, and went on to advance aquaculture techniques in China. After returning to Japan, he trained wakame farmers throughout the country, teaching them the horizontal longline cultivation method using bamboo floats.

As explained earlier, the use of kombu in the Ryukyu Islands is thought to have spread among commoners from the middle to the end of the Edo period. At that time, Hokkaido kombu was transported to Osaka by sea and thence down to Satsuma by land. It was shipped to China via the Ryukyu Kingdom as an important item of tributary trade. The inscription on the Bridge of Nations Bell continues as follows:

The Ryukyu Kingdom stands on an enchanted island between China and Japan. The Kingdom navigated ships to bridge all nations, filling its land with the precious goods and products of foreign lands.

Looking back at the history of kombu, we can feel both the anguish and hope of the Ryukyu Kingdom, which "navigated ships to bridge all nations."

14. Ōtsuki Yoshirō (1901–81): Graduated from the School of Fisheries Sciences of Hokkaido University and worked for the Asamushi Marine Biological Station (the present-day Research Center for Marine Biology, Tōhoku University). He was invited to Manchuria in 1929, when stock prices on Wall Street plunged, triggering the Great Depression worldwide. He worked in the Kwantung Experimental Fishery Station to cultivate kombu and wakame seaweed.

Seaweed · *Mō*

Mō seaweed is called *mōi* in Okinawa and *ibaranori* on the mainland. Like *kanten* (agar), *mōi* is high in carrageenan (an algae extract used as a thickener and stabilizer in many foods), so it is used to make *mōi dōfu*, a dish similar to aspic, with ingredients such as *kamaboko* steamed fish paste, carrots, and green peas. Nowadays in Okinawa, packaged dry *mōi* is available in the market. In the old days, however, Okinawan women used to collect it themselves from the sea during the spring, wading in up to their waists to make the harvest. They always kept a stock of dried *mōi* at home and rehydrated it as needed for cooking. When they made *mōi dōfu*, a special treat, proper molds were unavailable, so housewives used a rectangular lunch box to mold the jelly.

Mō is a red seaweed, *Hypnea charoides Lamouroux*. It is bitter and salty, makes the body cold, and is nontoxic.

Mō dissipates sluggish qi, brings down head lumps and swelling, eases abdominal pains caused by menstrual bleeding in women, promotes urination, and treats edema. It damages the spleen and stomach, so it should not be eaten daily.

Mōi dōfu

★ Ingredients
Mōi, *kamaboko* steamed fish paste, carrot, dashi stock, green peas, sugar, soy sauce, mirin, a little salt

★ Directions
Wash the *mōi* and soak in water. Dice the *kamaboko* and carrot finely and simmer in sugar and soy sauce until the carrot softens. Add the *mōi* to dashi stock, bring to a boil, and cook down until only a little liquid remains. When the *mōi* has dissolved, add the carrot, *kamaboko*, and seasonings. Cook until the liquid thickens, then remove from heat. Allow to cool and then pour into a mold.

Dried mōi (ibaranori)

Mozuku • *Sunori*

Sunori is mozuku (*Cladosiphon okamuranus*). It is salty, makes the body cold, and is nontoxic.
Sunori unclogs the throat, dissipates lumps, and promotes the discharge of moisture. It has the same effects as *mō* seaweed.

Sunori, called *sunui* in Okinawa, is a thick variety of *mozuku*, a type of edible seaweed. It grows on rocks in tropical water shallow enough for sunlight to penetrate. Like other types of seaweed, *sunui* grows in spring but dies out in summer when the water temperature rises. Where *sunui* grows naturally by the beach, locals call it "sea noodles" and eat it right out of the water after picking it and rinsing it in seawater—a method only possible in Okinawa. They say the slimy texture of the seaweed is particularly delicious. The slime contains anticancer agents. *Sunui* is cultivated widely in Okinawa, and is most often served as an *usachi* vinegared dish. The seaweed brings the flavor of the sea when used as an ingredient in miso soup, clear soup, or tempura.

Sunui tempura

★ **Ingredients**

Sunui, flour, egg, and water, plus extra flour for dredging, oil for deep-frying

★ **Directions**

Put *sunui* in a sieve and rinse under running water to remove some of the salt. Squeeze and cut into desired lengths. Combine egg, flour, and water to make a light batter. Dredge the *sunui* lightly in flour, dip in batter, and deep-fry.

Sunui usachi (vinegared *sunui*)

★ **Ingredients**

Sunui, seasoned vinegar, *tachibana* or *yuzu* citrus

★ **Directions**

Put *sunui* in a sieve and rinse under running water to remove some of the salt. Squeeze out water and cut into desired lengths. Dip in seasoned vinegar and serve. Add sliced *tachibana* or *yuzu* citrus as an aromatic garnish.

(Both the tempura and *usachi* recipes use salted *sunui*, which is how *sunui* is generally sold.)

Lichen • *Hatake-aosa*

Hatake-aosa, or *Nostoc commune,* is a lichen. It is bitter and cooling to the body, and is slightly toxic.

One theory holds that lichens are neutral and nontoxic. They clear the eyes and reduce heat in the internal organs. However, as lichens grow under moist conditions, consuming them in excess will damage the spleen and stomach. They should be avoided by frail people.

Tsūkan categorizes this lichen as a moss. However, lichens are not plants, but organisms resulting from a symbiotic relationship between algae and fungi. In Okinawa, this lichen is called *mōāsa*, *ishi-kurage* (stone jellyfish), *nenjumo*, or *juzumo*. Before World War II, locals used to braise it with tofu, put it in stacked boxes, and take it to celebrations. There is a seaweed with a similar name, *āsa*. To distinguish *āsa* from *mōāsa*, locals used to call the seaweed "sea *āsa*." After the war, however, the word "sea" was dropped because people stopped eating *mōāsa*, and there was no longer a need for the distinction.

Dried mōāsa

Mōāsa irichī

★ **Ingredients**

Mōāsa (lichen), carrot, green peas, shiitake mushrooms, *kamaboko* steamed fish paste, *ukara* tofu pulp, pork broth, sugar, soy sauce

★ **Directions**

Soak the *mōāsa* in water until soft, then cut it into small pieces. Stir-fry with the carrot, green peas or other greens, shiitake mushrooms, and *kamaboko*. Stir in the *ukara*. Add a small amount of pork broth and season with sugar and soy sauce.

Pork • *Buta-shishi*

Buta-shishi is pork meat (*Sus scrofa domesticus*). It is sour, cools the body, and is slightly toxic.

Pork replenishes weak kidney qi and cures chronic psychotic disorders. Long-term consumption blocks blood flow, weakens muscles and bones, and causes flabbiness. Pork also generates wind-dampness, causing various diseases. It should be avoided by those suffering from wind strokes, cold-damage diseases, and incisions. Boiling pork with *saikachi* fruits or jasmine tea detoxifies the meat, reducing the risk of disease. The fruit and tea also make the pork cook well.

Incompatible foods: Ginger, soba, whorled mallow, coriander, pickled plum, beef, mutton, egg, crucian carp, stir-fried beans, reindeer meat, turtle and softshell turtle, Japanese quail, bellflower, goldthread root, kutki root (Picrorhiza rhizome), Siberian cocklebur fruit, Euodia fruit, smoked black plum

Tsūkan writes that "boiling pork with *saikachi* fruits or jasmine tea detoxifies the meat." A note given in the reprint of *Gozen honzō* explains that the *saikachi* mentioned by Tsūkan is *Gleditsia japonica*, and its fruits have small, hard, chestnut-brown pods. *Saikachi* is a tall deciduous tree that grows naturally in fields and mountains. It bears tiny light-yellow flowers in summer and podded fruits in autumn. The pods contain flat seeds and grow to be 19 to 29 cm long. They are used to make herbal medicine or as a detergent for washing clothes.

Once, several years ago when I was feeling poorly, I canceled a trip to Okinawa. A friend of mine living on an isolated island sent me *saikachi*, telling me to make a decoction of it. I realized that Tsūkan's teachings, passed down orally through the generations, are alive today among the islanders of Okinawa.

Hanchumi *(On opposite page)*

★ Ingredients
Pork (lean meat), sugar, soy sauce, *awamori* rice liquor, ginger, dried bonito flakes

★ Directions
Hanchumi was made to preserve meat in the days before refrigeration. This traditional Okinawan shredded meat dish goes well with cooked rice. Chop the pork into bite-sized pieces. Lightly toast the bonito flakes. Combine the sugar, soy sauce, *awamori*, ginger, and bonito flakes in a pan. Bring to a boil, then add the pork pieces, place a drop-lid on top of the liquid, and simmer for a long time. When the meat is tender, remove from heat. Allow to cool, then shred with chopsticks.

Ina-muduchi *(Top right)*

★ Ingredients
Pork loin, yellow carrot, *kamaboko* steamed fish paste, *konnyaku*, dried mushrooms, dashi stock, light miso

★ Directions
Ina-muduchi means "pseudo-wild boar." It is a light-miso soup containing pork instead of wild boar meat, along with many other ingredients.
Briefly parboil thin slices of pork loin. Cut the carrot, *kamaboko*, *konnyaku*, and reconstituted dried mushrooms into rectangular slices. Dissolve the light miso in the dashi stock, add all other ingredients, and cook until vegetables are tender.

This soup is served to guests in winter. In summer, a clear soup called *shika-muduchi* (meaning pseudo-deer) is made using pork instead of venison.

Rafutē (slow-cooked pork) *(Above)*

★ Ingredients
Pork rib (skin on), *awamori* rice liquor or sake, sugar, soy sauce, dashi stock

★ Directions
Briefly parboil the pork rib. Tie the rib with string to shape it. Bring to a boil in a pot of water and *awamori* and cook for about two hours. Allow to cool. In a saucepan, combine the dashi stock with the sugar, soy sauce, and *awamori* and add the pork rib. Cover with a drop lid and simmer for about three hours over medium heat (slice the meat before simmering if desired). Remove from heat when the pork is well flavored and tender enough for a chopstick to slide through it. When cooled, take out the rib, cut the string, slice the meat as desired, and serve.

This recipe is good for making tasty *rafutē* at home. At my restaurant, we took an extra step. Right before serving, we heated the meat in a steamer, then put it on the plate and poured some of the cooking sauce over it.

Minudaru
(steamed pork)

Minudaru is steamed pork topped with a thick paste of black sesame seeds. Steaming gets rid of excess fat and gives the meat a lighter taste. The black sesame seed paste adds an appetizing aroma. *Minudaru* is an indispensable dish for the *tundābun* tray.

★ Ingredients
Pork rib (skin on), *awamori* rice liquor or sake, mirin, sugar, soy sauce, black sesame seeds

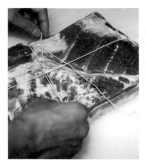

1

Tie the rib with string to shape it.

2

Place the rib on a cooking tray and sprinkle *awamori* on it.

3

Put it in a steamer and steam over medium heat for about 90 minutes.

4

Let cool and then cut the meat into slices.

5

Combine the mirin, sugar, soy sauce, and *awamori* or sake to make a marinade. Reserve a small amount to mix with the sesame seeds. Use the rest to marinate the slices in a cooking tray for a couple of hours.

6

Grind the black sesame seeds into a paste in a mortar.

9

Return the meat to the steamer and steam over medium heat for 5 to 10 minutes.

7

Season the sesame paste with the reserved marinade.

10

Cut into bite-sized pieces before serving.

11

Serve.

8

Spread the seasoned paste on each rib slice.

Leaf lard • *Buta-yu*

Buta-yu is leaf lard. It is sweet, makes the body slightly cold, and is nontoxic. Lard nourishes the stomach and intestines, promotes urination, treats jaundice and edema, makes hair grow, dissipates blood stasis, enhances blood vessels and veins, cures colds, moistens the lungs, and removes toxicity from vegetables and sulfur. Leaf lard is not simply fat rendered from the meat, but the fat in the belly that wraps around the internal organs such as the liver and intestines, both small and large.

In olden days when every Okinawan family had pigs, lard was carefully stored in an earthenware pot. A bit was scooped out to make all kinds of dishes. *Chinsukō* is a dry confection made with lard that resembles traditional Chinese cookies. Nowadays, this sweet is a typical souvenir of Okinawa. With its long shelf life, *chinsukō* is well suited to the tropical climate of Okinawa.

Chinsukō

★ Ingredients
Leaf lard, flour, sugar
★ Directions
Melt the lard in a pan. Add the flour and sugar and then stir well with a wooden spoon. Preheat the oven. Shape the dough into balls and put them on a baking tray. Bake until brown just as you would bake cookies.

Pork liver • *Buta-kimo*

Buta-kimo is pork liver. It is bitter, warms the body, and is nontoxic.

Pork liver controls children's seizures, warms internal organs that have cooled from fatigue, stops long-term illnesses caused by cold, halts uterine bleeding and vaginal discharge, replenishes the liver, and clears the vision. Pork liver cures edema caused by physical deterioration. However, when a pig is slaughtered, the shock it experiences goes into the liver and stays there. One should not eat too much pork heart and liver together. The liver should be avoided when taking medicine.

Incompatible foods: Raw fish and vegetables seasoned in vinegar, carp, Japanese quail

The underside of the lid of a lacquered bowl. Gold lacquer in relief depicts Shīsā, the guardian god of Okinawa.

Chimu-shinji

★ Ingredients
Pork liver, yellow carrot, dashi stock
★ Directions
Chimu means "liver," and *shinji* is "decoction." This soup is said to be good for people with bad eyesight or anemia.
Soak pork liver in water to remove the blood. Boil and cut into pieces of desired size. Chop carrot finely and add to the dashi stock with the liver. Simmer for a long time. Serve.

Chimu-yose

★ Ingredients
Pork liver, *kanten* agar, soy sauce, mirin, ginger, scallions
★ Directions
Soak pork liver in water to remove the blood. Boil, drain, and then push through a sieve to make a paste. Add soy sauce, mirin, and grated ginger. If using stick *kanten*, soak in water for 20 minutes, then bring to a boil. When the *kanten* dissolves, stir the solution into the seasoned liver paste and pour into a mold. Add chopped scallions, if desired, to remove the smell and add color.

Pork lung · *Buta-fuku*

Buta-fuku is pork lung. It is sweet, slightly cools the body, and is nontoxic.
To replenish the lungs and cure persistent coughs due to lung deficiencies, boil pork lung with sesame oil and eat. To cure bloody phlegm caused by lung deficiencies, boil pork lung with lotus seeds and eat. The cooking may be done in two ways. One is to boil in equal amounts of sake and water for night and day, and then add soy sauce. The other is to boil in water, cut into thin slices, and then simmer in goose broth. Remove the bubbly scum floating on the surface, as usual.

Incompatible food: Thick malt syrup

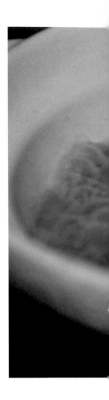

Pork heart · *Buta-fukumame*

Buta-fukumame is pork heart. It is sweet and salty, neutral, and nontoxic.
Pork heart alleviates shock, shakes off depression, stops palpitations, cures qi counterflow, and supplements blood deficiency. It treats paralysis after childbirth in women and sweating caused by bad temper in children. Pork heart replenishes the heart, but long-term consumption drains heart qi.

Pork kidney · *Buta-mame*

Buta-mame is pork kidney. It is sweet and salty, cools the body, and is nontoxic.
Pork kidney harmonizes the kidney, promotes urination, replenishes the bladder, warms the knees, treats deafness, improves the metabolism, strengthens qi, removes phlegm and clogging, reduces chills in the abdomen, cures gonorrhea in women, and stops vaginal discharge and bleeding after childbirth. Pork kidney strengthens the kidney, but long-term consumption causes deterioration of reproductive functions. To cook, boil it first and then add sake and soy sauce.
The longer pork kidney is simmered, the more tender it becomes. Cooking it with other ingredients reduces its flavor and increases its odor.

Pork stomach · *Buta-ohogai*

Buta-ohogai is pork stomach. It is sweet, warms the body slightly, and is nontoxic.

Pork stomach replenishes the internal organs, enhances qi, stops thirst, cures diarrhea caused by frailty, slows deterioration of the five internal organs, and removes the causes of illness. Eating balls of glutinous rice steamed with pork stomach treats fatigue and parasitosis in children. Daily consumption is good for people with deteriorating health or poor blood circulation due to internal heat. Pork stomach also reduces lumps and treats various sores.

Pork organ meats simmered in miso

★ Ingredients

Parboiled pork lung, heart, kidney, and stomach (these are often sold together at markets), miso, dashi stock, *awamori* rice liquor, soy sauce, scallions

★ Directions

Dissolve the miso in the dashi stock. Cut all of the organs into bite-sized pieces and add to the liquid. Simmer over medium heat until the organs are tender. Halfway through, season with a little *awamori* and soy sauce. Chop the scallions and sprinkle on top immediately before serving.

Pork intestines • *Buta-wata*

Buta-wata are pork intestines. They are sweet, and make the body slightly cold; they are nontoxic.

Pork intestines treat frequent urination due to abnormal thirst. They treat abnormal thirst originating in the lower abdomen, remove wind-heat from the small and large intestines, moisten the intestines, and relieve constipation. They relieve dysentery, hemorrhoids, and bloody bowel discharge.

Nakami-jiru
(clear soup with
pork entrails)

★ Ingredients
Pork entrails (including intestines), fresh ginger, dashi stock, *konnyaku*, shiitake mushrooms, salt, soy sauce

★ Directions
Combine chopped entrails and ginger with dashi stock and simmer until the entrails become soft. Add *konnyaku* and shiitake mushrooms, then season with a little salt and soy sauce. Chop young leaves from the Indian long pepper vine (if available) and sprinkle on top for flavoring.

Buta-wata, also called *nakami*, is a popular ingredient in typical Okinawan dishes featuring pig entrails. Today, pretreated entrails can be purchased at stores. When families had pigs, they cleaned the intestines at home—rubbing them with soy pulp or soybean skins, washing them thoroughly, and kneading them with salt before cooking. *Nakami-jiru* soup was often cooked for wedding celebrations and seasonal festivities.

Pig trotters • *Buta-ashi*

Buta-ashi are pig trotters. They are sweet and salty, cool the body slightly, and are nontoxic.

Pig trotters moisten the skin, increase breast milk, and reduce swelling. Trotters of female pigs are recommended. There are three ways to prepare trotters. One is to boil them in water, drain, and then simmer in 600 ml of sake and 54 ml of soy sauce, then add sun-dried tangerine peel and leeks. Another is to simmer in shrimp broth and add soy sauce. The third is to put the trotters in a jar with sake and soy sauce, and then immerse the jar in boiling water to cook them.

Buta-ashi are pig trotters—the part from the leg joint down to the hoof. This part is cut into round slices called *chimagū*. Pig trotters are stewed with daikon radish and kombu to make *tebichi* (simmered pig trotters), a special dish in Okinawa. The excerpt from *Gozen honzō* says pig trotters reduce swelling, moisten the skin, and help mothers with newborn babies have plenty of milk, so they are a desirable food for women. In Okinawa, senior citizens also love *tebichi*. It's a pity this dish is hardly ever served in mainland Japan.

Tsūkan explains three ways to boil trotters; these are almost the same as modern cooking methods.

Chimagū made from the front trotters is tasty but sinewy, so it is served to the young. *Chimagū* from the hind legs is tender and fattier, so it is served to the elderly.

Tebichi

★ **Ingredients**

Chimagū (sliced pig trotters; these can be found in Okinawan markets), kombu knots, daikon radish, dashi stock, *awamori* rice liquor, salt, soy sauce, Indian long pepper

★ **Directions**

Parboil the *chimagū* and drain. Put the *chimagū* in a deep pan with knots of kombu, daikon radish, and *awamori*. Simmer in plenty of water for several hours, skimming off scum gathered on the surface. When the liquid has cooked down, add the stock. Continue cooking until the meat can be easily separated from the bones, and then season with salt and soy sauce. Serve with a little cracked Indian long pepper on top.

Pig blood •*Buta-ketsu*

Buta-ketsu is pig blood. It is salty, neutral, and nontoxic.

Pig blood produces blood, reduces abdominal spasms and palpitations, and cures colds originating in foreign places. It also treats paralysis, headaches, and dizziness. To stop bloody bowel discharge, boil pig blood with sake and eat. To treat heartburn, boil in soy sauce and eat. Pig blood detoxifies various substances.

Incompatible foods: Rehmannia root, Chinese knotweed, yellow soybeans

Chi irichī, a pork dish cooked with pig blood, exhibits the true value of the Okinawan way of eating every part of the pig. Today, the blood of a freshly slaughtered pig is collected, steamed with salt and starch, and then preserved. Before World War II, however, pig blood was reportedly sold in a washbowl as-is. When fried, the blood produces an undefinably good flavor called *ajikūta* (meaning "plenty of unique flavor and taste") in an Okinawan dialect.

In Yamato, people long avoided meat because Buddhism taught that eating the flesh of a living creature caused defilement. Free from such notions, Okinawans cooked meat to make dishes indispensable for both celebrations and memorial services. In fact, the custom of consuming every part of the pig is widespread in Asia and Europe, where the food culture is carnivorous. Blood sausage, for example, is rather expensive in these regions. From this perspective, we could say that it was Yamato, not Okinawa, that was exceptional.

Chi irichī

★ **Ingredients**
Pig blood, pork rib, *kiriboshi daikon* dried daikon radish strips, dried shiitake mushrooms, *kamaboko* steamed fish paste, soy sauce, miso

★ **Directions**
Soak the dried shiitake mushrooms in water to reconstitute. Soak the dried daikon radish strips in water until soft, then squeeze out the liquid and set aside. Cut the pork rib, shiitake mushrooms, and *kamaboko* into rectangular slices, then braise in a deep frying pan, adding soy sauce and salt.
Mix the daikon radish with the pig blood and miso and add to the other ingredients. Cook over very low heat, stirring often, for a long time.

Pigs: Eat everything except the oink

Pork is the quintessential food of Okinawan cuisine. Records show that Okinawans had been raising pigs for four hundred years before pig breeding started on mainland Japan.[14] Okinawans eat every part of the pig—not only common cuts like pork roast, shoulder, and ribs, but also the legs, tail, head, entrails, and even the skin—cooking them in ingenious ways.

An old story says that locals anticipated the advent of the lunar New Year when they heard pigs squealing before they were slaughtered for festive dishes, and the animals' cries stimulated their appetite. It could be said that Okinawans relished even the squealing of pigs. Pork was a long-awaited New Year's delicacy and a treat served at annual seasonal festivals in Okinawa.

Since World War II, pigs are rarely kept in ordinary households. Instead, locals go to the market to buy pork, and the meat section is crowded with shoppers before the New Year. The year-end demand for pork exceeds supply from both Okinawa and the mainland, so some quantities are imported from overseas. I'd say Okinawans' love of pork is exceptional. However, a recent report[15] states that Naha ranks sixteenth in Japan in terms of pork consumption by household. This ranking surprised me, as I have long observed the lives and diet of Okinawans. I think the ranking must have been based only on the consumption of pork meat, excluding the trotters, tails, and entrails favored by the islanders.

In ancient times, people on the Okinawa Islands used to eat wild boar and dugong meat, as well as horsemeat and beef. When did they switch to eating pork almost exclusively? *The Okinawa daihyakka jiten, jō* (Okinawa encyclopedia, vol. 1) says, "Oxen and horses were important draft animals for farming and transport. Horses were also considered valuable as tributes or vehicles of privileged classes. For this reason, the slaughter of oxen and horses was prohibited." An ordinance issued by the Ryukyu royal government in 1697 stated, "Oxen are useful for farming. The government will forbid people to slaughter oxen and use the meat for festivities."

The royal government often issued such prohibitions, and tried to keep track of horses and oxen owned by ordinary households. However, the

---

14. *Richō jitsuroku Ryukyu shiryō* [Yijo Sillok annals of the Yi Dynasty, vol. 2], translated by Kadena Sōtoku (Kyūyō Kenkyūkai, 1972). This was a record kept by a Korean whose boat had drifted to Kume Island in 1456.
15. Ranking by prefectural capital (average of the periods from 2005 to 2007), *Family Income and Expenditure Survey* by the Statistics Bureau of Japan, Ministry of Internal Affairs and Communications.

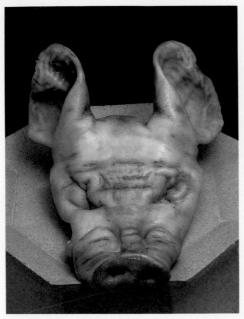

Chiragū *(skin from the head of a pig). "Eat every part of the pig except the oink." Okinawans waste no part of a pig, eating everything from head to foot. Chiragū, often served sliced and seasoned with vinegar, has a crunchy texture.*

prohibition orders included a clause that allowed people to slaughter an aged ox or horse provided that they reported the killing to authorities. The general populace may have gotten around the prohibition orders by taking advantage of such a clause—or the law may not have applied to them. According to *Yaeyama seikatsushi* (Yaeyama bionomics) written by Miyagi Aya, every family on the Yaeyama Islands used to make a rice gruel called "New Year's beef treat." Yaeyama is far away from the capital city of Shuri, so the islanders may have been exempt from the government law. Traditionally, families butchered an ox, pig, or goat several days in advance of a celebration and divided the meat equally among their neighbors. Words for this custom of sharing are still known to the islanders: *hanbun-wāki* (divide equally into two) and *mishi-waki* (divide equally into three).

In any case, royal government orders forbidding the killing of oxen and horses had a loophole, exhibiting some leeway typical of Okinawa, but pork gradually took center stage in Okinawa's carnivore culture. One reason for this was the influence of Chinese investiture envoys, according to the treatise *Ibunka tono sesshoku to juyō* (Contact with and acceptance of an alien culture).[17]

Investiture envoys are discussed in detail on pages 22 to 27. Every time a Ryukyu king acceded to the throne, the emperor of China sent envoys with imperial messages to recognize the king as the ruler. The Chinese mission comprised some hundred officials who stayed in the Ryukyus for several months

17. Kanashiro Sumiko, "Okinawa no nikushoku bunka ni kansuru ichi kōsatsu" [Study of Okinawa's carnivore culture], in *Ibunka tono sesshoku to juyō* [Contact with and acceptance of an alien culture], Yūzankaku Publishing, 1997. Reprinted in vol. 8 of *Zenshū Nihon no shokubunka* [Encyclopedia of Japanese food culture], edited by Haga Noboru and Ishikawa Hiroko.

at a time, causing an enormous financial burden on the economically strained royal government.

Sai On, a high-ranking official of the Ryukyu Kingdom, writes about pork for Chinese missions in his book *Hitori monogatari* (Soliloquy): "We needed twenty pigs a day but could not procure them solely inside the kingdom." To satisfy the appetite of investiture envoys, the royal government had to encourage the common people to keep pigs and forbade them to eat beef. This led to the development of the hog-raising industry. Also, under Chinese influence, people learned to cook pork by deep-frying and stir-frying, cooking styles that had been unfamiliar to them before. The government policy to promote pig breeding was also boosted by the sweet potatoes brought from China and cultivated widely as a famine food. Sweet potatoes were good fodder for pigs and made the breeding easy.

The *agū*, a breed of black pig raised as livestock in the Ryukyu period, has recently been drawing attention as a native island breed. It was thought to have become extinct during World War II. However, a few were found to survive, and the breed has been promoted recently. *Agū* meat is becoming popular for its rich flavor and lower cholesterol content, although the breed is still relatively rare. These days, the mainstay of the Okinawa hog industry is the prolific Yorkshire pig, a breed that first arrived in the form of postwar recovery gifts from Okinawans who had immigrated to Hawaii before the war.

People on mainland Japan eat only pork meat, but Okinawans eat every part of the pig, wasting nothing of its life.

Chiragū *Piglet seller, in* Ryukyu fūzoku ezu *(Ryukyuan manners and customs, illustrated). Courtesy of Sakamaki/Hawley Collection, University of Hawaii at Manoa.*

Goat •*Hitsuji*

***Hitsuji* is goat meat (*Ovis aries*). It is bitter, heats the body, and is nontoxic.**
Goat meat replenishes the internal organs, enhances qi, relaxes the
mind, reduces anxiety, and relieves pain. It may be eaten by pregnant
women. It treats dizziness, emaciation, damage to the five organs
and seven emotions in men, and fright-induced seizures in children.
It opens the stomach, and increases strength and reproductive
power in men. However, eating it after contracting a fever or an
infectious disease will always cause one to run a temperature, leading
to serious problems. Goat meat should not be cooked in a copper pan,
because this damages men's reproductive functions and causes women to
bleed unexpectedly. To cook, simmer goat meat with mushrooms and taro and
season with sake and soy sauce.

*Incompatible foods: Plums, green beans, tofu, soba, vinegar-pickled vegetables,
wild boar meat, sushi, vinegar*

Goat liver •*Hitsuji no kimo*

***Hitsuji no kimo* is goat liver. It is bitter, makes the body cold, and is nontoxic.**
Goat liver replenishes the liver, cures heat deficiency caused by liver wind, and assuages
painful eye infections. It is good medicine for people who have gone blind after running a
fever. However, pregnant women should avoid eating it because it will make their babies
prone to illness.

Incompatible foods: Raw Japanese peppers, bamboo shoots, plums, adzuki beans

Goat lung •*Hitsuji no fuku*

***Hitsuji no fuku* is goat lung. It is sweet, warms the body, and is nontoxic.**
Goat lung replenishes the lungs and reduces fatigue caused by coughing. It replenishes
deficiencies, treats colds, improves the qi of the lungs, promotes urination, and removes
various toxins. However, goat lungs contain worms from March to May. Remove the
worms before eating as they will cause diarrhea.

Goat kidney · *Hitsuji no mame*

Hitsuji no mame is goat kidney. It is sweet and nontoxic.
Goat kidney replenishes weak qi of the kidney, empowers the spirit, cures deafness caused by kidney deficiency and weak yin, and increases men's reproductive power. It strengthens the stomach, reduces urinary frequency, and stops night sweats caused by deterioration of the five internal organs.

Goat stomach · *Hitsuji no ohogai*

Hitsuji no ohogai is goat stomach. It is sweet, warms the body, and is nontoxic.
Goat stomach treats vomiting, halts sweating, and reduces thirst and frequent urination. Long-term consumption increases men's reproductive power, but can cause cancer of the esophagus.

Hijā (goat meat) soup

★ **Ingredients**
Goat meat, *fūchiba* (Japanese mugwort), salt, ginger

★ **Directions**
Boil chopped goat meat in a pot full of water until tender. Skim off scum that gathers on the surface. Halfway through, add plenty of *fūchiba* to remove the smell. Season with salt and ginger.

Goats are called *hijā* in Okinawa. Before World War II, every family had two or three goats. The animal was valued for its restorative properties, as indicated by the old saying, "A goat is medicine." Goat meat was also a delicacy to be served during festivities such as a celebration of the construction of a new house. Additionally, it was recommended as a nourishing food for pregnant women. *Hijā* soup, made after slaughtering a goat, was a delicacy that was served to show hospitality.

Kikigaki Okinawa no shokuji (Oral recollections: Okinawan cuisine) describes the slaughter of a goat in Yanbaru, the northern part of Okinawa's main island:

> When a goat 18 to 30 kg in weight is slaughtered, the body is hung with the head down and the hind legs tied to the branch of a tree. The carotid artery is slashed to collect blood in a wooden tub set underneath. The goat hide is burned until the skin is scorched. Then four or five men carry the goat to the beach and butcher it. The entrails are removed and slashed lengthwise and washed thoroughly. To remove the gamey smell, they are kneaded with soy pulp, washed again, and then boiled.

Those men must have made a fire in the field or on the beach and boiled the goat meat in a big pan. Reading this description, I could almost hear the joyful voices of men drinking *awamori* while waiting for the meat to cook.

Silver-stripe round herring • *Soreru*

Soreru is silver-stripe round herring (*Spratelloides gracilis*). It is sweet, neutral, and nontoxic.
Silver-stripe round herring eases the internal organs and makes the spleen and stomach healthy when eaten in soup (a hot, clear soup containing greens and meat). The effects are the same as those of glassfish.

Peanut-coated, deep-fried
sururu

★ **Ingredients**
Sururu (silver-stripe round herring), flour, eggs, crushed peanuts, oil for deep-frying

★ **Directions**
Make a batter from the flour and eggs, adding water if necessary. Dip the *sururu* in the batter, coat with crushed peanuts, and then deep-fry.

Silver-stripe round herring is called *sururu* in an Okinawan dialect. Tsūkan says they have the same effects as glassfish, and recommends eating them in soup. Coating the fish with crushed peanut powder and deep-frying also makes a tasty, aromatic dish.

Okinawa is surrounded by the sea. In olden days, women went into the water at low tide. They made stone walls in a shoal and put bark of the *iju* (an evergreen tree with the Latin name *Schima wallichii*) or black-eyed-pea pods in the water to attract fish. With this device, women easily caught a large number of small fish, such as silver-stripe round herring and mottled spinefoot. They never had trouble obtaining ingredients to make stock for miso soup.

Sururu

Colorful fish at Naha's city market

Porcupinefish • *Abasu*

***Abasu* is porcupinefish (*Diodon holocanthus*). It is slightly sweet, neutral, and nontoxic.**

Porcupinefish replenishes the five internal organs. It warms the body and has a light taste. It is good for all kinds of illness.

Porcupinefish is called *abasa* in Okinawa and *harisenbon* (thousand needles) in mainland Japan. Porcupinefish are covered in spikes and inflate their bodies like blowfish when they sense predators nearby. Porcupinefish live in tropical waters, so they die when the water temperature drops. They look like blowfish, but they do not contain the same deadly toxin, so they do not require a license for preparation. After removing the spiny skin, the meat is deep-fried or used as an ingredient for a one-pot meal or miso soup.

Broadclub cuttlefish · *Kubushime*

Kubushime is broadclub cuttlefish (*Sepia latimanus*). It is sour, neutral, and nontoxic.

Broadclub cuttlefish increases qi, strengthens will, and promotes menstruation. Best suited for women after childbirth and individuals with poor blood circulation.

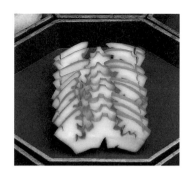

Kubushime in Okinawa is often introduced as the common cuttlefish in the order *Sepiida*. However, *kubushime* is larger, and is different from other types of cuttlefish. It lives in the shallow waters of the coral reef area in the southwest Okinawan islands. Fishermen catch it with a fishgig, diving with no tanks or snorkels. As the catch is small, *kubushime* is expensive; it is also called "phantom cuttlefish." The meat is thick and soft. It makes tasty sashimi and is also used to make flowered squid, a dish indispensable for *tundābun* (see pages 4 and 5).

Flowered squid

★ **Ingredients**
Kubushime, red food coloring or other red dyeing agent such as *akabana* flowers (*Epilobium pyrricholophum*) or roselle

★ **Directions**
Slice thick *kubushime* flesh into rectangles. Make cuts in the rectangles to create a flower-like shape. Boil the red coloring agent in water and add the cuttlefish to dye the flesh. When it is cool, cut into slices of desired thickness. Serve with vinegar and soy sauce.

Abasa soup *(On opposite page, top)*

★ **Ingredients**
Abasa (porcupinefish), miso, dashi stock, scallion or fennel fronds

★ **Directions**
Peel the skin of *abasa* with pliers (use them to break the spikes). Chop the meat into large chunks and parboil. Dissolve miso in dashi stock, add *abasa* and simmer. Add fennel to remove the fishy smell. If fennel is not available, sprinkle thin strips of scallion on top immediately before serving.

Erabu eel • *Irabū unagi*

**Irabū unagi, or Laticauda
semifasciata, is an Erabu eel.
It is salty, neutral, and
nontoxic.**

Erabu eels get rid of pains
in the head, eyes, mouth,
and teeth. They are used to
treat various illnesses after
childbirth, cure dysentery and
white diarrhea, stop bleeding
due to parasites, treat various
types of bad incisions, remove
wind-dampness, stop pain,
and warm blood to improve
the flow of meridians. They
are a medicine for paralysis,
cold and moisture, and
are effective as a *choketsu*
medication for women
following childbirth.

Smoked irabū

Irabū or *irabu*, a sea snake, is also called "Erabu
eel" because it lives in the seas off Erabu Island. In
Okinawa, dishes made with *irabū* have long been
considered a special nourishing food. On Kudaka
Island, only family members of Shinto priests
called *noro* were allowed to catch the sea snake.

Smoked *irabū* is sold in the market, either
pulled straight like a stick or coiled like a hose.
Irabū shinji is broth made by boiling *irabū* for a
long time. It is served to mothers during recovery
from childbirth and valued as a tonic for men.

Kamaboko steamed fish paste • *Kamaboku*

Kamaboku is steamed fish paste.

The effects of this food depend on the nature of fish used to make it, but all types of fish are moderate and do no harm to patients of various diseases. One may eat *kamaboko* anytime. Broth may be served as soup for frail or chronically ill individuals.

Kamaboko, or *kamaboku*, used to be homemade; it was a way of preserving fish. When there was a large catch or fish prices were low, locals made *kamaboko* quickly while the fish was fresh, as if to compete against time. They were proud of making *kamaboko* that stayed good for a full week.

To make *kamaboko*, filleted white-meat fish is carefully skinned and boned. The fish meat is chopped and then pounded until it becomes sticky, and other ingredients are added. The resulting paste is neatly shaped before being boiled or steamed.

Kamaboko

★ Ingredients

White-meat fish (e.g., *gurukun* banana fish), salt, sugar, mirin, egg white, potato starch (or corn starch or other powdered cooking starch)

★ Directions

Fillet the fish. Peel off the skin and carefully remove the bones and dark flesh. Chop the meat finely with a knife. Pound in a mortar until sticky (or use a blender or food processor). Add the salt, sugar, mirin, egg white, and starch powder to the sticky fish paste and mix well. A small amount of ground taro makes it tastier. Shape the paste with wet hands on a thin board or tray lined with kombu. Place in a hot steamer and allow to steam until the paste solidifies. Steaming time will vary with volume; check after about 30 minutes.

Irabū shinji, simmered *irabū*

★ Ingredients

Irabū sea snake, rice bran, kombu, *chimagū* pig trotters, salt, soy sauce

★ Directions

Irabū shinji:

Char the skin of *irabū* over an open fire. Coat it with rice bran and rub with a scrubber to wash well. Cut *irabū* into appropriate lengths. Arrange the pieces in a bundle like firewood, wrap in a sheet of kombu, and tie with string. Boil in a pot full of water for five to six hours, removing the scum that rises to the surface. When the liquid is reduced to one third, remove from heat and strain the broth. This soup is called *irabū shinji* and taken as is as a medicine.

Simmered irabū:

Cut the ventral side (where there are no scales) of an *irabū* prepared as when making *irabū shinji*. Remove the guts and bones. Use *irabū shinji* as stock. Add the *irabū* meat, pig trotter, and knots of kombu. Simmer for several hours until the pig trotter is tender. Season with salt and soy sauce. This traditional dish is considered richly flavored haute cuisine.

Gazami crab • *Gazame*

Gazame is the *gazami* crab (*Portunus trituberculatus*). It is salty, neutral, and nontoxic.

Gazame removes pathogenic heat in the chest, reduces blood clots, relieves pain, reduces twitching lips and face swelling, cures lacquer poisoning, nourishes muscles, strengthens qi, lets qi flow through the meridians, and helps digestion. Eating *gazame* with vinegar is good for the joints. *Gazame* is also beneficial because it reduces vexing heat in the five internal organs. Crabs often have toxins, but not *gazame*. It may be eaten by anyone, including sick people.

The reprint of *Gozen honzō* adds another description: *Gazame is also called gazami. . . . This is a type of crab that lives in the sea. When boiled, the crab turns a beautiful red.*

In regions outside Okinawa, *gazami* refers to the blue crab found off the coasts of Japan's mainland—from the northern part of the main island to Kyushu—as well as Korea and the northern region of China. The blue crab is one of the delicacies of winter.

The Okinawan *gazami* is different from the blue crab. Its shell has serrated edges, so it is sometimes referred to as the *nokogiri* (sawtooth) *gazami*. This crab comes into season in summer. As described in the reprint, *gazami* turns a pretty red when boiled and has a unique sweet taste.

These crabs live in mud holes under mangrove trees or in mangrove forests, so they are also called mangrove crabs or mud crabs.

Fresh gazami

The right and left claws are different sizes, and are strong enough to crack hard objects. The meat in these claws is delicious.

Today, *gazami* crabs are farmed in the brackish waters at the mouths of tropical waterways. People in Tsūkan's time would not have dreamed of such an undertaking.

How to eat *gazami*

Boil fresh *gazami* in salted water. Serve with a flavored vinegar, such as vinegar mixed with soy sauce or sesame oil. The crabmeat may also be chopped up and stir-fried or used as an ingredient in miso soup.

Fruits

Public market in Naha

Gozen honzō has entries on twenty-six types of fruits and sweets (including crystallized sugar) and their effects, but only a few of them are introduced in this book. In Shuri Castle, as many as sixteen fruits and sweet desserts were served during receptions for Chinese investiture envoys. Meanwhile, the nameless masses of the Ryukyus—constantly struggling to survive famine and natural disasters—most likely never saw the peaches and grapes described in *Gozen honzō*.

Luckily, the tropical soil produced a variety of wild fruits from season to season. *Kikigaki Okinawa no shokuji* (Oral recollections: The diet of people in Okinawa), compiled in 1988, gives us a glimpse of the lives of twentieth-century Okinawans:

> Oleasters, wild strawberries, *ginma* [a shrub producing small purple fruits], *tekachi* [*Rhaphiolepis umbellate*], and *achikunnai* [*Berchemia lineata*] grew wild and bore copious amounts of fruit. Children knew exactly when and where to find them. They also knew the right time for eating them. Children had to do chores such as weeding and collecting firewood, but they got together on their way to pick and eat fruits of the season. After eating *ginma* or *Berchemia lineata* fruits, the children's mouths, hands, and even clothes were all stained purple.

Tangerine seller, Ryukyu fūzoku ezu (*Ryukyuan manners and customs, illustrated*)
Courtesy of the Sakamaki and Hawley Collection, University of Hawaii at Manoa

130

Lychee · *Leiki*

Leiki (*Litchi chinensis*) is a lychee. It is sweet, neutral, and nontoxic.

The lychee is a tall evergreen tree of the soapberry family. It is native to China. The fruit resembles longan fruit. The rough outside of the fruit has a turtle-shell pattern. The flesh is eaten as food or used as a medicine. It assuages thirst, enhances the complexion, and strengthens qi. Eating *leiki* in excess, however, produces a deficiency of heat.

Lychee is known as the favorite fruit of Yang Guifei, who was the favored wife of Emperor Xuanzong of Tang-dynasty China. The emperor is said to have had lychees delivered to his beloved by horse over a distance of more than ten thousand kilometers. The translucent white flesh is sweet, and can be eaten without cooking. Lychees are also preserved in syrup or used to make lychee juice or liqueur.

Longan · *Ryugan*

Ryugan (Dimocarpus longan) is a longan. It is sweet, neutral, and nontoxic.

Ryugan, or longan, is a tall evergreen tree of the soapberry family. The fruit is round, and the brown hull has fine patterns. The seed, similar to that of a loquat, sits in the flesh, which is called longan meat. Longan fruit is eaten as food or used as a medicine. It replenishes the heart, improves intelligence, nourishes the stomach, strengthens the spleen, cures amnesia and palpitations, and calms the mind to bring a deep sleep. The longan improves judgment and the ability to concentrate, and treats diseases that damage and cause deficiencies in the heart-spleen.

A longan has white, sweet, and faintly aromatic flesh like a lychee. It is eaten raw or preserved in syrup. Dried longan meat is a herbal medicine that contains many vitamins and minerals.

Shīkuwāshā · *Tachibana*

Tachibana is suikwāshā (*Citrus depressa*). It is sweet and sour, warms the body, and is nontoxic.

Suikwāshā is a tree in the *Rutaceae* (citrus) family. The flesh is eaten as food, and the peel is used as a medicine. *Suikwāshā* relieves thirst, opens the stomach, and lets qi in the chest flow. When sweet, the fruit moistens the lungs; when sour, it collects phlegm. The peel halts vomiting, gets rid of phlegm, stops coughing, and detoxifies liquor. The fruit freshens fishy breath.

Incompatible food: Mud crab

Shīkuwāsā, also called *hirami* lemon, grows in Amami Oshima, Okinawa, and Taiwan. *Shī* means sour, and *kuwāsā* means something to eat, as well as to wash. In ancient times, cloth made from Japanese banana fiber was soaked in *shīkuwāsā* juice overnight and then washed in the river. The name of the fruit is said to have come from this custom.

Banana · *Baseo no mi*

Baseo no mi is banana (*Musa balbisiana*). It is sweet, makes the body very cold, and is nontoxic.

Baseo no mi means the fruit of *baseo*—the banana plant. When eaten raw, it halts thirst, moistens the lungs, and heals bleeding incisions. It detoxifies liquor and gets rid of pathogenic heat in children. Dried banana lowers skin fever and reduces vexing heat.

Note: Dried *baseo* is made by pickling bananas in plum juice and pressing them flat when dried. Bananas can be toxic: unripe green bananas, bananas that fall to the ground, twin bananas that are undeveloped, and bananas that sink in water or change colors quickly are all dangerous. Eating them is fatal, so one must be prudent.

Baseo no mi, the banana, grows naturally in tropical regions in Asia and Africa. A large quantity is cultivated for eating raw or in cooking. Bananas native to Okinawa are rather small, resembling miniature bananas. They are mostly eaten raw but are sometimes deep-fried. Unpeeled bananas can also be roasted in a covered pan. The dried *baseo* mentioned by Tsūkan is probably today's equivalent of banana chips. According to the excerpt, chips were made after pickling bananas in plum juice.

Even today, we should heed Tsūkan's advice. He warns against eating bananas that have fallen, bananas that are undeveloped doubles or are discolored, and bananas that sink in water.

Roasted bananas

Sugarcane
• *Ogi*

Ogi is sugarcane (*Saccharum officinarum*). It is sweet, neutral, and nontoxic.

Sugarcane is a perennial grass in the Poaceae family. Called *ogi* in Okinawa, it is prized as highly as other fruits. It makes qi flow, harmonizes the internal organs, enhances qi of the spleen, benefits the small and large intestines, gets rid of phlegm, relieves thirst, removes burning sensations from the chest, detoxifies liquor, halts vomiting, and improves digestion. Sugarcane cures stomach reflux and eases the thorax.

Sugarcane originated in New Guinea. It was brought as medicine to Yamato in 754 by the Chinese monk Ganjin. *Ryukyu rekishi yawa* (Notes on Ryukyu history) written by Minamoto Takeo contains a section on the cultural history of unrefined sugar:

> On November 21, 754, a second Japanese envoy ship coming back from Tang-dynasty China stopped over in Okinawa. On board were deputy ambassador Ōtomono Komaro and the Chinese monk Ganjin. A record says the ship also carried eighty bundles of sugarcane.

I assume this was not the first shipment of sugarcane to Okinawa. Sugar refining was introduced to Tang China from India. Ryukyuans seem to have learned it from people in Fujian, China with whom they had close ties.

To make brown sugar, sugarcane is crushed to produce juice. The collected juice is then heated and concentrated until it becomes solid.

Never-ending sugarcane fields in the southern part of Okinawa's main island

Afterword

Tokashiki Pēchin Tsūkan wrote *Gozen honzō* at the end of the Edo period. Printing techniques such as woodblock printing had not been introduced to the Ryukyus yet, so transcription was the only way to make copies. According to research by Yokoyama Manabu,[1] six transcribed copies are known to exist. Two of the six are in the library collection of the University of Hawaii. One is the Nakagusuku-bon; it is in the oldest format and bears the ownership stamp "Nakagusuku Palace," indicating that it was the property of the Ryukyu royal government. The other is the Sueyoshi-bon, which bears the ownership stamp of one Mōsei Sueyoshi.

Another three, named Kō, Otsu, and Hei, are in the Higashionna Kanjun collection of the Okinawa Prefectural Library. The existence of the last copy, known as the Murano-bon, is referenced only as a record in the library catalog of medicinal herb researcher Murano Tokiya. The catalog contains an entry that says, "*Gozen honzō* (new transcript), one copy, Tenpo Year 6, Tokashiki Pēchin Tsūkan."

In writing this book I referred to two reprinted editions, which I placed on the right and left sides of my desk. One was the *Gozen honzō* reproduced by Yokoyama Manabu, who compared the five existing copies and used the Nakagusuku-bon as reference. The other was the reprint compiled by Tōma Kiyohiro and published in 1964. Tōma does not mention which copy of *Gozen honzō* he used for reprinting.

These two references—Yokoyama's reproduction and Tōma's reprint—differed in several aspects, including the descriptions and the number and order of entries. These differences are thought to have occurred in the process of transcription. I studied the differences and decided on which versions to use for each entry in this book.

I am not a research specialist, so I struggled hard with the archaic writing. But I experienced great joy as the ancient practices began to slowly make sense to me. My horizons expanded as I learned how ancient Ryukyuans leading humble lives had pursued such noble interests. I was fascinated by the image of artless people who respected nature despite exposure to its violent forces, and who lived together with their gods. I had to remind myself again and again that I was writing a cookbook, and forced myself to return to writing about food ingredients.

---

1. *Zōho: Ryukyu-koku shokuryōsho Gozen honzō* [Addition: The edible plants of Ryukyu] (Nakagusuku Edition, vol. 1) published by Seikatsu Bunka Kenkyūjo Nenpō in 1987.

Gozen honzō was written for the palace kitchen staff and presented to the king. But was it written only for the king's cooks (*hōchū*), who were in a privileged class? The cooks probably wouldn't have needed all of the cooking directions and explanations in the Ryukyu dialect. *Gozen honzō* comprises a mixture of entries on expensive foods from China and Yamato cooked in the palace kitchen and ordinary foods that would have appeared on the tables of commoners. Such contradictory elements make me think that Tsūkan must have been looking beyond the palace to the masses living outside of its walls.

While writing this book, I received advice and assistance from a number of people. Mr. Ōmine Jissei made Ryukyuan-style plates and bowls for me at the Yomitan Kitagama kiln. Professor Emeritus Shō Hiroko of the University of the Ryukyus kindly gave me access to documents on Baron Shō Jun. I would like to express my sincere gratitude to professors emeriti of Okinawan studies Takara Kurayoshi and Kaneshiro Sumiko; the staff of the Okinawa Foundation, the Naha City Museum of History, and the Okinawa Prefectural Library; Mr. and Mrs. Yoshido of Kanpōdō Fine Arts; and many other people who told me about the lives of prewar Okinawans. Last but not least, I offer cordial thanks to Ms. Akiyama Reiko of the Tonbo-no-hon editorial team, who encouraged me and pointed me in the right direction whenever I was in doubt.

Bibliography

Akamine Masanobu, comp. *Okinawa no kami to shoku no bunka* [Okinawan gods and food culture]. Tokyo: Seishun Publishing, 2003.

Arai Hakuseki. *Nantōshi gendaigo yaku* [Modern translation of Nantōshi with annotations]. Translated and annotated by Harada Nobuo. Ginowan: Yōjusha, 1996.

Arashiro Toshiaki. *Kōtōgakkō Ryukyu Okinawa shi* [Okinawan and Ryukyuan history for high school]. Itoman: Toyo Planning and Printing, 2001.

Go Keishi. *Yakuchū shitsumon honzō* [Translation and annotations of *Shitsumon honzō*]. Translated and annotated by Harada Nobuo. Ginowan: Yōjushorin, 2002.

Goldschmidt, Richard. *Neu-Japan* [The New Japan]. Berlin: J. Springer, 1927.

Haga Noboru and Ishikawa Hiroko, comp. *Zenshū Nihon no shokubunka dai 8 kan: Ibunka tono sesshoku to juyō* [Encyclopedia of Japanese food culture vol. 8: Contact with and acceptance of an alien culture]. Tokyo: Yuzankaku Publishing, 1997.

Hatsushima Yoshihiko and Amano Tetsuo. *Ryukyu shokubutsu mokuroku* [A catalog of Ryukyuan plants]. Naha: Deigo Shuppansha, 1977.

Hawley Collection Compilation Committee, comp. *Hōreisōkan dai 5-shū: Ryukyu fūzoku ezu.* [Hawley collection vol. 5: Okinawan manners and customs illustrated]. With contributions by Sa Hiretsu and Uezu Hitoshi. Tokyo: Honpō Shoseki, 1982.

Henshū Iinkai, ed. "Nihon no shokuseikatsu zenshū Okinawa." In *Nihon no shokuseikatsu zenshū vol. 47: Kikigaki Okinawa no shokuji* [Collection of articles on the Japanese diet, vol. 47: Meals in Okinawa based upon oral recollections]. Tokyo: Rural Culture Association Japan, 1988.

Hokama Shuzen, annotator. *Omorosōshi jō ge* [Ancient Ryukyu epic poems, vols. 1 and 2]. Tokyo: Iwanami Shoten, Publishers, 2000.

Iha Fuyū. *Okinawa rekishi monogatari: Nihon no shukuzu* [A tale of Okinawan history: A microcosm of Japan]. Tokyo: Heibonsha, 1998.

——*Ko Ryukyu* [Old Ryukyu]. Edited by Hokama Shuzen. Tokyo: Iwanami Shoten, Publishers, 2000.

Jo Hokō. *Chūzan denshinroku.* [Record of transmitted facts of Chūzan]. Translated and annotated by Harada Nobuo. Ginowan: Yōjushorin, 1999.

Kadogami Shūei. *Gozaibansama shōsei no toki zenbu nikki ni tsuite* [Notes on the banquet menu]. Naha: Okinawa Prefectural Library private edition, 1992.

Kamakura Yoshitarō, ed. *Ko Ryukyu bingata* [Old Ryukyu bingata textiles]. Kyoto: Kyoto Shoin, 1974.

Kaneshiro Sumiko. *Miyaradunchi Ishigakidunchi no zenfu nikki: Kinsei Okinawa no ryōri kenkyū shiryō* [A record of the meals served at the residences of Miyaradunchi and Ishigakidunchi: Historical material on cooking in early-modern Okinawa]. Fukuoka: Kyushu University Press, 1995.

Kobakura Yasuyoshi. *Ryōri Okinawa monogatari* [Okinawa through food]. Tokyo: Sakuhinsha, 1983.

Matsuyama goten monogatari kankōkai, ed. *Machiyama udun monogatari: Meiji Taishō Shōwa no Matsuyama goten no kiroku* [The Story of Matsuyama Palace: Records from the Meiji, Taishō, and Shōwa periods]. Naha: Shō Hiroko, Borderink, 2002.

Minamoto Takeo. *Ryukyu rekishi yawa: Ryukyu rekishi no uramen o kaimei suru* [Notes on Ryukyu history: Unraveling the other side of Ryukyu history]. Naha: Okinawa Bunkyo Shuppan, 1971.

Miyagi Aya. *Yaeyama seikatsushi* [Yaeyama bionomics]. Naha: Okinawa Times, 1972.

Miyamoto Tsuneichi. *Nihon minshū-shi 7: Kansho no rekishi* [Japanese popular history vol. 7: The history of sweet potatoes]. Tokyo: Miraisha, 1962.

Naka Shōhachirō. *Okinawa Amami no bunken kara mita kurozatō no rekishi* [The history of unrefined sugar from Okinawa and Amami documents]. Naha: Borderink, 2003.

Naruse Uhei, Takeda Masatsune, Iizuka Muneo, eds. *Shinpan shokuzai zuten seisenshokuzai hen* [New edition: Encyclopedia of food, volume on perishables]. Tokyo: Shogakukan, 2003.

Niijima Masako. *Watashi no Ryukyu ryōri* [My Ryukyu dishes]. Tokyo: Shibatashoten, 1983.

Ryukyu Shimpo, ed. *Shin Ryukyushi: Kinsei hen jō* [New history of Ryukyu: Modern era, vol. 1]. Naha: Ryukyu Shimpo, 1989.

——*Shin Ryukyushi: Kinsei hen ge* [New history of Ryukyu: Modern era, vol. 2]. Naha: Ryukyu Shimpo, 1990.

Takara Kurayoshi. *Ryukyu ōkoku* [The Ryukyu kingdom]. Tokyo: Iwanami Shoten, Publishers, 1993.

——*Okinawa rekishi monogatari zoku* [The story of Okinawan history, second series]. Naha: Hirugisha, 1986.

Tōma Kiyohiro, ed. *Gozen honzō* [Edible plants of Ryukyu]. Naha: Tōma Kiyohiro, 1964.

Tomiyama Kazuyuki, ed. *Nihon no jidaishi 18: Ryukyu Okinawa-shi no sekai* [Japanese history 18: The historical world of Ryukyu and Okinawa]. Tokyo: Yoshikawa Koubunkan, 2003.

Uezato Takashi. *Me kara uroko no Ryukyu Okinawa-shi saishin rekishi koramu* [Surprising facts on Ryukuan and Okinawan history: The latest historical information]. Naha: Borderink, 2007.

Wakasa Yoshihiko. *Ryukyu shuyō yakuyō shokubutsu* [Main medicinal plants of Ryukyu]. Naha: Asahidō Insatsujo, 1953.

Yamazato Eikichi, ed. *Matsuyama ōji Shō Jun ikō* [Posthumous writings by Prince Matsuyama Shō Jun]. Tokyo: Shō Jun Posthumous Manuscripts Publishing Committee, 1969.

Yanagita Kunio. *Kaijō no michi* [The ocean route]. Tokyo: Chikumashobo, 1967.

——*Kainan shōki* [Notes on the southern sea]. Tokyo: Kadokawa, 1956.

Yokoyama Manabu. "Ryukyukoku shokuryōsho *Gozen honzō*" [Ryukyuan food treatment book *Gozen honzō*]. In *Seikatsu bunka kenkyūjo nenpō* [Research institute for culture and cultural history], vol. 1. Okayama: Research Institute for Culture and Cultural History, Notre Dame Seishin University, 1987.

——"Ryukyukoku shokuryōsho *Gozen honzō* sakuin" [Index of Ryukyuan food treatment book *Gozen honzō*]. In *Seikatsu bunka kenkyūjo nenpō* [Research institute for culture and cultural history], vol. 2. Okayama: Research Institute for Culture and Cultural History, Notre Dame Seishin University, 1988.

——*Ryukyukoku shisetsu torai no kenkyū* [A study of Chinese investiture envoys to Ryukyu]. Tokyo: Yoshikawa Koubunkan, 1987.

Yonami Takeo. *Shin Ryukyu ōtōshi 16: Shō Kō Ō* [New history of Ryukyuan royal descendants vol. 16: King Shō Kō]. Naha: Shinsei Shuppan, 2006.

PUBLIC DOCUMENTS, REPORTS, AND MAGAZINES

Genji gannen shina sappōshi rairyū shoki gekan [Visit of the Chinese investiture envoy to Japan in Genji year 1, vol. 2]. Nakahara Zenchū Collection.

Izenasonshi Henshū Iinkai, ed. *Izenasonshi chūkan: Shima no komonjo* [History of Izena village, vol. 2: The island's ancient documents]. Izenasonshi Henshū Iinkai, 1988.

Naha Shisei 70 Shūnen Kinen Kikaku Jikkō Iinkai, ed. *Rekishi o hiraku: Ryukyu bunka hihō ten* [Exhibition: Looking into history: The secret treasures of Ryukyu culture]. Naha: Naha City, 1991.

Nahashi Keizai Bunkabu Rekishi Shiryōshitsu, ed. *Nahashishi shiryō hen dai1-kan 9, kinsei Naha kankei shiryō: Ryukyu shiryō kanbun hen* [History of Naha city, documents, vol. 1, chap. 9: Documents on early-modern Naha and Ryukyu written in classical Chinese]. Naha: Naha City, 1998.

Nahashi Kikakubu Bunka Shinkōka, ed. *Nahashishi shiryō hen dai 1-kan 11: Ryukyu shiryō ge* [History of Naha city, documents, vol. 1, chap. 11: Documents on Ryukyu, second volume]. Naha: Naha City, 1991.

Nahashi Kikakubu Shishi Henshū Shitsu, ed. *Nahashishi shiryō hen dai 2-kan chū no 7 Naha no minzoku* [History of Naha city, documents, vol. 2, chaps. 2–7, folk customs of Naha]. Naha: Naha City, 1979.

"Ryukyu Yakuzen: Ōke no Shoku Yōjō" [Yakuzen Chinese Herbal Medicine Dishes in Ryukyu: The Medicinal Food of the Royal Family]. *Okinawa ni sumu* [Living in Okinawa] (magazine), February 2008.

Takigawa Yoshikazu. "*Chūzan denshinroku* Bussan Kō no Ichi Kōsatsu" [Examining the Treatise on the Products and Specialties Mentioned in *Chūzan denshiroku*]. *Journal of Ryukyuan Studies* 61 (2003).

"Tokushū Okinawa" [Special feature: Okinawa]. *Taiyō* [Sun] (magazine), September 1970.

"Tokushū Okinawa o Tabe Tsukusu" [Special Feature: Eating up Okinawa Food]. *Taiyō* [Sun] (magazine), April 1994.

About the author

Takagi Rin, a native of Tokyo, is an acclaimed screenwriter for television and radio dramas. Her works have received many prizes, including the Grand Award in the prestigious Galaxy Awards.

She first connected with Okinawa when she took a break from her intense work schedule to visit the islands. During her stay there, she developed a deep appreciation for the Okinawan people and their culture—especially the food. This passion led to a new phase in her life: in 1998 she opened a restaurant serving traditional Okinawan food in Akasaka, Tokyo. Her interest continued with several writing projects focusing on various aspects of Okinawa. One of these, the biography *Okinawa dokuritsu o yume mita densetsu no joketsu Teruya Toshiko* (Teruya Toshiko, the brave woman who dreamed of an independent Okinawa), took the Grand Prix in the fourteenth Shogakukan Non-Fiction Awards.

Takagi now lives in Kanagawa Prefecture, where she runs a café.

About the translators

Enda Kazuko is a Japanese translator who lives in Tokyo. Her recent works include a writing textbook for Japanese readers called *Ultimate English Writing* and a co-translation of Okamoto Ryosuke's *Pilgrims in the Secular Age: From El Camino to Anime* and Saito Hiroshi's *Rudolf and Ippai Attena*.

Deborah Iwabuchi is a US-born translator who lives in Gunma Prefecture. Her recent translations include Takagi Nobuko's *Translucent Tree* and a co-translation of Okamoto Ryosuke's *Pilgrims in the Secular Age: From El Camino to Anime* and Saito Hiroshi's *Rudolf and Ippai Attena*.